The Wanderer

For Kingsley

THE WANDERER
THE STORY OF FRANK SOO

by Susan Gardiner

ELECTRIC BLUE PUBLISHING
2016

First published 2016.

Electric Blue Publishing
Stowmarket
Suffolk, IP14 5AE

www.electric-blue.co.uk

Copyright © Susan Gardiner, 2016

The right of Susan Gardiner to be identified as the Author of the work has been asserted in accordance with the Copyrights, Designs and Patents Act 1988.

ISBN 978-0-9955396-0-0 (hardcover)
ISBN 978-0-9955396-1-7 (paperback)
ISBN 978-0-9955396-2-4 (ebook epub)
ISBN 978-0-9955396-3-1 (ebook PDF)

CONTENTS

ACKNOWLEDGEMENTS

I would like to thank the Soo family, particularly Jacqui Soo, Christian Hill, John Soo, Becky Soo and Lydia Soo.

I would also like to thank Alan Zheng-Phoon Lau for his wonderful support for this book and the following people who have helped and encouraged me along the way:

Elise Aasen, Chris Brader, Joe Byatt, Shaun Campbell, Alan Chadwick, Anna Chen, Sammy Chung, Neville Evans (National Football Collection), Pat Fryer, Daryl Goh, Stephen Guy (West Derby Society), Christine Hanefalk, Hyder Jawád, Chun Wing Lee, Anne Reekie, Paul Robinson, Lisa Scott-Lee, David Selby, Adam Sutch (RAF Museum, Cosford), Graham Taylor, Nigel Utting, Glyn Williams, Albert Au Yeung, Chris Yuen.

I am also grateful to the staff of the Staffordshire Sentinel, the English National Football Archive, the Britiah Newspaper Archive and the Record Office of Leicestershire, Leicester and Rutland.

The photographs have been very kindly supplied to me by John Soo, Jacqui Soo and Christian Hill. The front cover image and two other photographs are reproduced with the kind permission of Staffordshire Sentinel News & Media. I would particularly like to thank Neville Evans of the National Football Collection for allowing me to use several images (including the back cover image) from Neil Franklin's scrapbook.

A NOTE ON NAMES

Frank Soo was always just Frank Soo. He was recorded as Frank Soo on his birth certificate and remained that on his marriage certificate and death certificate. The only variation of his name that I have ever come across is that many of his friends called him Frankie.

There has been a great deal of confusion about Frank Soo's identity because somehow he was incorrectly identified as Hong Ying or Hong Y Soo. There was indeed a (female) person of that name who was born in Liverpool in 1914, the same year that Frank Soo was born in Derbyshire. Because Frank moved to Liverpool as a child - we know that he arrived there some time before 1920 because his brother Ronnie was born there - it is quite easy to make the assumption that this was the future professional footballer, but like all his five brothers and one sister, Frank Soo was given a Christian name to go with his Chinese surname and baptized in a Church of England church, in his case, St Peter's, Fairfield. He was never called Hong Y Soo, or any variation of that name. Unfortunately this error has been repeated in many books and on many websites.

Frank Soo's career was reported on by several newspapers in Asia, including in Hong Kong. They used a Chinese name for him, Soo (or Su) Wai-ching.

On early documents, Frank's father's name appears as Ah Kwong Soo, or variations thereof. Later he appears to have adopted the simpler form, Quan Soo, and that appears as his full name on all documents from his later life. However, on his gravestone - he was buried next to his wife, Beatrice, in the Chinese section of Anfield Cemetery, Liverpool - the inscription is in both English and the Chinese language, pinyin. Chris Yuen has kindly helped to translate the inscription which also gives some invaluable details of where in China Quan originated (see Chapter 1):

> 區 Ou [surname]
> 君仕 Jun Shi [given name]
> 公 Esquire

I have called Frank's wife Freda throughout the book. This was her middle name, but it was the name she was known by to both her family and friends.

THE WANDERER

... him an exile's track awaits, not twisted gold;
a trembling body, not earth's riches;

...

As when he ere at times
in former days, his gifts enjoy'd;
then wakes again the friendless mortal

...

Then are the heavier his wounds of heart
painful after dreaming;

Anonymous Anglo-Saxon poem, written before 1072; translated by Benjamin Thorpe (1842)

FOREWORD
BY JACQUI SOO

Scousers. We are incredibly proud of our heritage. Home to the world's first elevated electric railway, affectionately known as the "Docker's Umbrella". The world's first scheduled transatlantic passenger service started by Samuel Cunard in 1840, the world's first school for deaf people and many more world firsts: first public baths and wash houses, medical officer of health, paid nurses to the poor, nursing school, public library, railway timetable. You get the picture? We are good at being The First.

Liverpool is home to the oldest Chinese community in Europe and home to Frank Soo, the first non-white man to play football for England. He was my great uncle.

Growing up in the sixties in Kirkby with a Chinese surname brought its challenges. But when I was informed by my Dad and Granddad that I had an uncle who played football for England and other football clubs, it gave me an immense sense of pride. Our whole extended family has been quietly proud of Frank in a typically, under-stated, humble kind of Chinese way. Only with the internet and the discovery that many people had not recorded his details correctly, or that he was never even mentioned in football annals, did this become very annoying.

I was alerted to the author's attempts to find out about Frank by a Stoke supporting friend. And the journey of discovery began. On behalf of the Soo family, I would like to thank the author for her tenacity in writing the story of this truly wonderful gentleman and trailblazer.

Jacqui Soo
Great niece of Frank Soo.

INTRODUCTION

On 14 October 1944, Frank Soo, England international, stood on the pitch at Wembley Stadium waiting for the referee to blow his whistle and start the match he was about to play in. The wartime international against Scotland would raise £23,000 for the Red Cross, a figure that would be worth well over half a million pounds today. Minutes before, the England players had lined up to be presented to King Haakon of Norway. Now, as Soo looked around the field, he could see his teammates, including the captain, Stanley Matthews and the two great Everton players, Joe Mercer and Tommy Lawton. Lawton, described in one obituary as "the princeliest, the most complete, simply the best centre forward in Britain," would score a hat-trick in this match in front of 90,000 football-starved spectators. It is not difficult to imagine the emotions that thirty-year-old Frank Soo must have felt as he stood on the Wembley turf, finally - and rightly - recognized as the equal of England's brightest footballing talents, playing at the highest level, and representing his country at a time when it was still at war. It must have been a remarkable feeling for someone who had grown up living above his parents' laundry business in Liverpool.

Only a fortnight before, Frank had played in a similar match at the Parc des Princes in Paris for an FA Services XI. The British side had won 0-5 but the result hardly mattered. The significance of a football match being played in a country only recently liberated from Nazi tyranny, between a French national side and a team representing some of its chief liberators was immense and it is unlikely to have been lost on the players, most of whom were still serving in the armed forces themselves. Whether these were the proudest moments of Frank Soo's career as a professional footballer it is impossible to say, but they must surely have been among them.

Frank Soo's presence in an England international side had additional significance, however, because he was the first footballer of Chinese or Asian ancestry to play for England. In fact, arguably, he was the first England international from any ethnic minority background, the first "person of colour," to use an expression that Frank would probably not have recognized himself. Before his time, there had been a small number of professional footballers who came from different racial backgrounds. Rab Howell (1867-1937), the Sheffield United, Liverpool and Preston North End player, came from a Romani background and won two England caps in the 1890s. Although he has been described as being "of full gypsy blood," it is difficult to establish Howell's ethnic origins and he was certainly

European. The Ghanaian-born goalkeeper, Arthur Wharton (1865-1930), was the first black professional footballer in the world and Walter Tull (1888-1918), who was of mixed race, played for Tottenham Hotspur and Northampton Town, before being killed in action in France in 1918. Both of these men were important figures in the sport but neither of them played international football. Frank Soo played in nine matches for his national team between 1942 and 1945 in what were known as Wartime or Victory Internationals. Sadly, none of Frank's England appearances have been recognized as official caps, a decision that many prominent people in football have publicly criticized, including the former England captain (and the man who would replace Soo in the England side in 1946), Billy Wright.

Whether or not his status as a representative of an ethnic minority was of the same importance to Frank himself, or to his contemporaries, is uncertain. His was an age when footballers did not generally see themselves as role models or influential figures in society, although a few players did become very famous and in some cases were adored by supporters. Today, *galácticos* like David Beckham often publish more than one book before their playing careers are over, whereas it was unusual during the period between the first and second world wars for footballers to write about themselves in what were, perhaps, less individualistic times. Whatever Frank Soo felt about his pioneering achievements as the first England international of Chinese origin - and he remains the only one to this day - he rarely expressed his thoughts on the subject publicly, although in an interview that he gave in 1975, long after his playing days were over, he told the Stoke-on-Trent newspaper, the *Evening Sentinel*, that he felt that he "would have had many more [England appearances] but for his Oriental blood."

Until 1939, the press coverage of Frank Soo's career almost invariably referred to his Chinese background. He was "the Chinaman," "the Chinese player," or "the Oriental" and bad puns about firecrackers and wordplay using his name featured in almost every item about him ("Soo Soon," "To See Soo," "Soo Suits" and so on). In all the press coverage of his playing career in England, though, there does not seem to have been anything that was openly hostile towards him on racial grounds, at least judging by what is still available today. Members of Frank's family believe that his England career ended after a racist cartoon, depicting Frank dressed as a Chinese "coolie" and implying that he should not have been picked for England, appeared in a newspaper, and although family stories can often be surprisingly accurate – and I believe that this one is true - there is unfortunately no trace of the cartoon. Generally, Frank Soo received very positive press coverage even in the early days of his professional career. His photogenic good looks ensured that his image appeared everywhere, often accompanying match reports in which he wasn't even mentioned. He had that intangible thing, "star quality" or charisma, on and off the pitch, and it was recognized even in the days when he was winning the admiration of the legendary Dixie Dean, who watched him playing for Liverpool schoolboys and who would recall the experience in his syndicated newspaper column in 1933: "It seems a pity such a striking personality and such a nice lad should have to go out of his own city to get his chance to appear in big football. I notice that Stoke have made him into a forward, whereas he was a wing-half-back all the time I ever saw him play with the schoolboys."

Dean was not the only one to lament Liverpool's profligacy with the youthful Soo's talents, and also spotted what would become a perennial problem: where to play him? His comments are typical of attitudes to Frank from the very beginning of his career. He was nice, likeable, charming. He impressed people with his personality, as well as his undoubted prowess on the football field. If there were any racial hostility, it vanished in the face of his commitment, his immense personal charm and his shining ability as a footballer and all-round sportsman. So most of the references to the fact that Frank was Chinese were probably only because it was seen as a genuine novelty and a bit of a landmark in football. A Dundee newspaper, the *Evening Telegraph*, regarded his debut for Stoke City in 1933 as headline news:

CHINESE PLAYER TO TURN OUT IN ENGLAND

Frank Soo, a 19-year-old Chinese footballer, who is to play for Stoke City against Middlesbrough on Saturday, will be the first Chinese to play in English League football. He is an inside-left, and when he steps on the field at Middlesbrough will realize the ambition of his life, for since a small boy he has been a keen player.

This report is typical of the coverage of Frank Soo's early career and references to his ethnicity would continue to appear in the press until the Second World War, when attitudes towards him seem to have changed somewhat. Influenced perhaps by his enlistment in the Royal Air Force and selection as an England international, there were fewer allusions to Frank's Chinese origins in the post-war period. From then onwards, he would most often be described as an "England international" and by 1945, it was quite usual for him to be referred to as "the Stoke City, England and RAF player."

In doing the research for this biography, I've read countless books about the period when Frank Soo was at the height of his fame as a professional footballer. Books about football, biographies of players and autobiographies by players that were both teammates and friends, even books about the Football Association and the Football Players' Union.

It was rare that I came across even a mention of Frank Soo's name. Only Joe Mercer and Neil Franklin (whose career at Stoke City briefly overlapped with the end of Frank's and who played with him for England during the Second World War) mention him at any length. This is in such great contrast with contemporary newspaper coverage. It would not be too great an exaggeration to have called him "a household name" or a "star" at that time. It is genuinely difficult to understand how or why Frank Soo has all-but-disappeared from football history. He was, by all accounts, a popular player in the dressing–room, loved and admired by football fans at every club he played for, a constant presence in newspapers throughout his career as a player, and later, when he was a coach and manager. Soo's many years living abroad certainly contributed to this. When he returned to live in England in the 1980s, the football world had changed dramatically, and he was a forgotten man. Perhaps if he had managed for a longer time in England, like Joe Mercer or Stan Cullis, things might have been different. It does not explain his "disappearance" completely, however, and the reader must decide what the other reasons for this were.

I chose to call this book *The Wanderer* not because Frank Soo had any particular association with the many football clubs that use the name, but because his story reminded me of an Anglo-Saxon poem with that title. Written at least seven hundred years before Frank Soo was born, it is in part a lament. The Wanderer is in a kind of exile, far away from his family, his friends and his home. He finds no comfort as he travels the icy seas of northern Europe. He wonders what has become of the things he used to know, the glorious days of his youth and the companions he shared them with. He attempts to reconcile his sadness with resignation, loyalty, generosity and courage. These are all characteristics that made Frank Soo the person he was. In his later years, he cuts a rather lonely figure, but it is clear that he took great comfort from memories of his achievements in the game he loved and the many years he was able to spend passing on his immense artistry and skill to several generations of younger players.

When I began writing about Frank Soo, I believed that it was important that his place in football history as a player of Chinese ethnic origin should be recognized. Now that I know the story of Frank Soo's life and career in more detail, I am certain that his qualities as a supremely accomplished player, a role model, and a human being who overcame great obstacles to become one of the great talents of European football, have earned him a place alongside the other great stars of his time, regardless of his origins. I hope that this book will help to restore him to his rightful place as an important figure in the history of the game.

1

'IT WAS UNFORGIVEABLE NOT TO TRY'
Buxton, Sheffield, Liverpool, 1914 - 1932

Frank Soo was born on 8 March 1914 at 17 Victoria Terrace, Fairfield Road, in the small Derbyshire parish of Fairfield, which is now part of the larger spa town of Buxton. His parents were Quan and Beatrice Soo. They had been married at St Luke's Church in the Chorlton-upon-Medlock area of south Manchester in 1908. Frank's mother, whose family name was originally Whittam, was probably from Salford or Pendleton in Lancashire. Quan Soo, a laundry proprietor, was born in about 1884 in China and his marriage certificate gives his late father's (and therefore Frank's grandfather's) name as Cooi Quan, a farmer. It's most likely that Quan Soo's family worked some kind of smallholding. Farms in late nineteenth-century China were on average only three acres, and often only one acre, in size. Many young Chinese men left their country in an attempt to escape a life of poverty and hardship. Most of them worked their passage across to England, sometimes via the United States, as merchant seamen and, according to Frank's nephew, John Soo, "Frank's father came from Canton (Guangzhou) in China when he was very young. Over the years he was looked after by the Chinese community in Manchester. That's where he met his wife, an English girl."

A translation of the inscription on Quan and Beatrice's grave, which is in the Chinese section of Anfield Cemetery in Liverpool, gives more detail of where in Guangzhou Quan came from. A translation of it reveals that he came from Donghu village, in or near the town of Chishui, Kaiping County in Guangdong Province. An article about Frank Soo in a Hong Kong Chinese-language newspaper, the *Sing Tao Jih Pao*, said that his ancestors came from Chungshan (which is now spelt as Zhongshan, a city in the Guangdong Province close to both the city of Guangzhou (Canton) and Kaiping).

The early background of this "English girl," Frank's mother, Beatrice, is no easier to trace than the Chinese ancestors on his father's side and is even more mysterious. According to her marriage certificate, she was born in 1888, the daughter of Walter Whittam, a railway clerk, who – like Quan's father – was dead by the time of their marriage. However, the only child called Beatrice Whittam whose birth was registered with the General

7

Record Office between 1886 and 1889 was the daughter of a dressmaker, Ruth Whittam, born in Salford on 2 April 1888. There are no details of a father on the certificate, and the baptism register of St Bartholomew's church in Salford, describes Ruth Whittam as a spinster living at 51 Ellor Street, Pendleton. If this is the child that grew up to be Frank Soo's mother - and although it is impossible to prove that she is, it seems likely - records tell us that she had a harrowing early life, eventually being admitted to the Manchester Industrial School for Girls in Sale, where her record states that she had been badly neglected, that her mother denied that Beatrice was her child and had put her out to be nursed, at the age of five weeks old, by another woman, a Mrs Hulley, who was living at 1 Dalton Street, Salford. Sarah Hulley, and her husband John, had treated the child so badly that she was removed from their care by the recently-established National Society for the Prevention of Cruelty to Children (NSPCC). The notes on her admission document stated: "Child does not know Mrs Lund [Ruth Whittam, who had married and changed her name to Sarah Lund] is her mother, has been taught to call her aunt and denied it in Court." Beatrice had been "charged" with "wandering, having no people, [or] guardianship" and was to be detained until the age of sixteen. It was quite common at this time for girls from this kind of background to be sent to work in laundries. Whatever her origins, at the time of her marriage to Quan in 1908, Beatrice was living at the same address as him, at 60 Downing Street, Chorlton-upon-Medlock, where Quan was described by the registrar of marriage as a laundry proprietor.

Frank Soo was not the only professional footballer to have been born in Fairfield. George Kitchen, who would play in goal for Everton, West Ham and Southampton, had also been born in the same village thirty-eight years earlier. Kitchen is very much a local surname in the Peak District, and there were many members of that family among the quarrymen and agricultural labourers of the Derbyshire moorlands. Frank, on the other hand, appears to have been born in this beautiful but remote area by chance, his parents having moved there shortly before he was born. It's possible that relatives on Frank's mother's side of the family were living in Fairfield already – a Whittam family was living in Fairfield Road in 1911 – or it may simply have been that Fairfield was one of the nearest places to Manchester without a Chinese laundry, thereby creating an opportunity for the young Soo family to earn a decent living and have a better quality of life. There was certainly plenty of competition for this kind of business in Manchester at that time as the city had a total of 351 Chinese laundries in 1911. This was despite a very small number of Chinese-born people being resident in England and Wales at that time. The census records only 1,319 in total, all but eighty-seven of them male. The Chinese laundry appears to have been the main way that Chinese people were able to earn a living in early twentieth-century Britain, much as the Chinese takeaway was towards the end of the century. So much so that in 1932 the famous Lancashire-born music hall performer and film star, George Formby, had a huge hit with a comic song called *Chinese Laundry Blues*, about the lovelorn Mr Wu. It was stereotyping on a grand scale, albeit affectionate, but demonstrates what an integral part of working-class culture the Chinese laundry had become at that time.

Another possible reason for the family to have moved away from Manchester was because of the increasing animosity towards Chinese immigrants during this period. The hostility was greatest in urban areas and in the north west of England, where many Chinese seamen had settled. In Liverpool, the resentment had reached such a point that it threatened to turn into serious social unrest. Many of the Chinese men who had moved there at the end of the nineteenth century and the years before the First World War had found work in the docks, which resulted in protests against them – most vociferously by trade unions – and Chinese labour became a major issue in that area in the 1906 General Election causing socialist writer, Graham Wallas, to comment that "anyone who saw much of politics in the winter of 1905/6 must have noticed that the pictures of Chinamen on the hoardings aroused among many of the voters, an immediate hatred of the Mongolian racial type." Just as they are now, in the twenty-first century, politicians back then were unscrupulous in their use of immigrant workers as scapegoats - and there is an uncanny similarity in the attitudes that left Chinese workers trapped in a double bind of prejudice to those faced by immigrants today. If they worked hard, they were taking "local" people's jobs and undercutting wages. If they didn't have work, they were lazy and possibly even criminal. It was a no-win situation and life must have been very difficult for anyone starting out with a young family, as Quan and Beatrice were. The following item, published in the *Manchester Courier and Lancashire General Advertiser* on 4 December 1906, shows the attitude of some people in the region towards Chinese immigrants at around the time of Quan and Beatrice's marriage:

The Central Council of the Liverpool Working Men's Conservative Association, last evening, indignantly denounced the influx of Chinese into the city. Mr. Thomas Atkinson, vice-chairman, and a Labour magistrate, said these foreigners were sweaters, and deprived Englishmen of employment and livelihood. Mr. T. Garrett, member of the Liverpool Select Vestry, said the Guardians [who ran the workhouses] had to maintain many indigent foreigners and therefore to increase the rates. Mr. J. Scott said the Chinese, by working for low wages, often really drove our own people into the workhouse. Men working at the docks knew they were coming in daily by twos and threes. Mr. Joseph Ashcroft... urged the boycotting of

Chinese laundries, declaring: 'If you can kill the soap combine, you can kill these Chinese.'

This was not moderate language and it must have been very worrying for members of the small Chinese community who had settled in the area. In addition to this, the Chinese were also subject to accusations of criminality, dishonesty, and in some cases, involvement in opium dealing. Stories such as the one reported in the *Manchester Courier* on 8 April 1913, the year before Frank Soo was born, were common. Describing the trial of a number of Chinese men following a police raid on a laundry in Chorlton-upon-Medlock, which was allegedly used as a front for illegal gambling, its headline told readers of a "motley crowd of Oriental figures in the dock." The reporter also managed to find time to have some fun mocking the defendants' names. A Sheffield newspaper report of the same case, mentioned, without irony, that the men were all very well dressed, "despite the fact that they were all laundrymen."

Just as much of a threat, in the view of some at least, was that Chinese men were regarded as being sexually rapacious or, even worse, attractive to local women. Relationships between immigrant Chinese men and Lancashire women were clearly also a cause of resentment. For many working-class women in Liverpool and Manchester, the prospect of marriage to a hard-working man from the Chinese community was more appealing than becoming involved with the sometimes drunken, violent alternatives on offer in their local area, but there were serious drawbacks to such relationships. In a letter to the Home Office in 1906, the Chief Constable of Liverpool wrote: "There is, no doubt, a strong feeling of objection to the idea of the half caste population which is resulting from the marriage of English women to the Chinese." White women who married Chinese men in this period were widely regarded as "low," promiscuous and thought to be involved with illegal drugs, gambling and prostitution. Many were even shunned by their own families. Women who were British nationals and became the wives of immigrants automatically lost their nationality and became aliens upon marriage, under legislation such as the Aliens Act of 1905, further cutting them off from the mainstream of society. Of course, the marriage of Frank's parents may have a simple explanation and they probably married for the same reasons that most couples do. They certainly had a long and apparently happy marriage, which produced six sons and a daughter, and ended only with the death of Beatrice in 1954.

This was the atmosphere into which Frank Soo and his brothers and sister would be born. Urban Lancashire in the early twentieth century was not an encouraging environment in which to bring up mixed-race children and it seems quite probable that Quan and Beatrice's move to rural Derbyshire may partly have been an attempt to escape such tensions. Already in the trade, and therefore with the knowledge of how it was all done to the high standards that would be expected by their customers, a laundry was the obvious choice for the young couple. It may have been that Quan had been a laundryman in the merchant navy on his journey from China to England. It was how many Chinese immigrants started out. Besides, laundries in England had traditionally been run, and often quite badly run, by women and that meant that their Chinese counterparts were not competing with the bigger, exclusively male, industries where unionized workers dominated. By doing what was considered to be "women's work," Chinese laundrymen avoided accusations of undercutting other men's jobs at a time when trade unions were actively trying to close down the immigrant-run businesses that they felt threatened the livelihoods of their members.

The Chinese were often the first community to be attacked whenever there was anti-immigrant tension in Britain. In 1911, less than three years after Quan and Beatrice's wedding, there were serious outbreaks of violence in Wales and the north west of England. Gangs of youths stoned Chinese-owned homes and businesses, smashing windows and worse. The violence was particularly bad in Cardiff where a bake-house where Chinese people had taken refuge was set on fire and burned out and there were similar incidents in Lancashire. It must have seemed like a good time for the Soo family to move out to the remote, wild and very beautiful Peak District village of Fairfield.

The tiny terraced house in which the family were living when Frank was born – Frank's older brother Norman had been born in Manchester in 1909 – was also the premises of the family business, a laundry called Jack China's. On Norman's birth certificate, his father was named as "Jack Soo," and it may be that Quan was sometimes called Jack by his family and friends. He appears as Quan (or variants of Quan, both government registrars and clergymen struggled with Chinese names at this time) on most subsequent official records, but a few local people in Liverpool, for example, have referred to "Jack Soo's laundry" in their reminiscences of the West Derby business that the family ran for many years. He was also referred to as Mr Jack Soo in the report of Frank's wedding that appeared in the Singapore newspaper, the *Straits Times*, in 1938. Jack was also the given name of one of his sons.

Frank and his family were not to remain in Derbyshire for very long. By the time that the Soo's next child – Frank's only sister, Phyllis Beatrice, usually known as Beattie – was born in June 1918, the family was living in Sheffield. In 1919, according to White's Trade Directory, the house in which Phyllis was born, 231 Crookes, was a laundry owned by Lee Sing. Whether or not they were working for someone else, or were just using another name, or the business had already been handed on to another proprietor by that time, is uncertain. It was around this time that the Soo family returned to the north west of England and finally settled in Liverpool where several of their descendants still live today. By the time Frank's brother Ronald was born, on 22 October 1920, the family were living at 10 Town Row in the West Derby district of Liverpool. This was to be their home for many years to come.

At this time West Derby was a suburban area of semi-detached houses, parades of shops and wide, leafy roads. Historically, the area had been a rural one, with parks, large country houses and, in Town Row itself, thatched cottages. The nineteenth century had seen some development, but there were still parks, such as Larkhill Gardens, farms, lawn tennis clubs and cricket grounds in the area. Contemporary photographs of West Derby show smart avenues lined with trees, and parts of West Derby were still quite rural by the time the Soo family moved there. A photograph taken in 1917 shows fields of marigolds next to West Derby Farm, with further fields and extensive farmland beyond. There would have been plenty of places for young, energetic children, like the Soo family, to play.

Their laundry and home was next to a small public house, the Royal Oak, and Lee's milk-house and dairy. It was certainly one of the more pleasant parts of Liverpool to grow up in, but there was also deprivation and poverty behind the respectable surface. On 2 March 1922, the *Times* reported that "at a meeting of the West Derby (Liverpool) Guardians yesterday it was stated that the number of poor receiving outdoor relief [the equivalent then of 'the dole' or welfare benefits] was 64,411, against 10,682 last year." This seems an extraordinarily high figure even for an urban area. There was clearly a great deal of poverty in West Derby and it is easy to imagine that Beatrice and Quan had to work extremely hard to bring up their seven children there, particularly during the depression of the 1920s and 1930s. The presence in their own locality of West Derby Union Workhouse, and various industrial schools and orphanages where the children of the poor were set to work, would have been a constant reminder to the seven Soo children of the need for hard work and discipline in life. There's little doubt that the reputation Frank had later in life, as a coach in Italy and Scandinavia, when he was known as a hard taskmaster, a man who expected complete commitment, self-discipline and energy from his players - as well as from himself right up until he was in his sixties - was schooled in the family laundry at 10 Town Row.

The writer Anna Chen devoted one episode (Programme 4: Steam and Starch) of her radio documentary series, *The Chinese in Britain* to the experience of growing up and working in a Chinese laundry. She pointed out that during the first half of the twentieth century, the only place "ordinary people all over Britain" were likely to meet a Chinese person was in a laundry. Her interviewees vividly remembered the noise, heat and steam of their family businesses, which in most cases was also their home. "Men would do washing while there would be a counter at the front 'probably staffed by a white woman.' " Above the laundry would be sewing rooms, and the family would live behind, sometimes with workers' bedrooms above.

In a BBC history project about life in Britain around the time of the Second World War, the unrelated Frank Wing Yow Soo recalled his life growing up in such an establishment in Cheltenham:

> I remember the laundry had a great big cauldron, about five feet across and heated by a coke fire underneath. All the dirty clothes were piled in and boiled, before being transferred to a large wooden tub for rinsing. The clothes were then spun dry in a 'hydro' and then transferred to the 'drying room' with wires strung across the ceiling.
>
> The room was heated by an iron coke stove which was also the heater for the flat irons. The flat irons were more versatile than the electric irons available then. In fact, stiff collars could only be formed or shaped with a flat iron - electric irons were too bulky and couldn't get hot enough. Only Chinese laundries were able to produce the very stiff collars as preferred by the police and armed forces and for formal dress wear.

No doubt the Soo family business was a similar set-up. It would have been noisy, steamy and oppressively hot and the hours were inhumanly long. In *The Chinese in Britain*, Olga Adderton recalled growing up in a household which would not have been so very different from the Soo home:

> The shop was open from very early to seven o'clock at night; the only day of rest was Sunday. ... They got up very early in the morning. Dad was always up about five o'clock. Mum would get up a little bit later. The beginning of the week was the washing of the clothes, sorting out first of all, putting them into piles of colours, whites, very dark things, and then they would do the washing Monday, Tuesday. By Wednesday, after the drying period, which was again late into the night, sometimes Dad would be going to bed about three in the morning, just to finish off and that he'd be up again at five. ... When the machines were on, you'd have this hot tub smell and steam, lots of steam, which used to go all through the house, always very sort of noisy with the machines and all and it was very hot.

Town Row was a relatively comfortable part of West Derby and the residents were mostly skilled workers or the owners of small businesses. They were shopkeepers, joiners or building contractors, or – in a few cases – comfortably off enough to be "living on their own means." 10 Town Row was already a Chinese laundry in 1911, long before the Soo family moved there, and was owned by Guangzhou-born Sam Chin, assisted by twenty-one-year-old Sam See, also from Guangzhou. Stephen Guy, chairman of the West Derby Society in 2014, recalls the laundry in West Derby village in the 1960s (probably after Quan's death in 1962): "Passengers on the top decks of buses could see the staff ironing." Others remember "Lee's Chinese Laundry" at that address. A local history, *The People of West Derby* describes it at an earlier date: "The establishment was one of a pair of shops opposite the Village Hall on Town Row. It was later occupied by Soo, also a Chinese laundryman. The front door to the shop opened onto Town Row; and about a yard inside could be seen the familiar figure of Mr. Soo, ironing shirts at his table."

10 Town Row was close to St Mary's church, the new parish church for West Derby, designed by the famous architect George Gilbert Scott and consecrated in 1856, where Ronnie (1920), Jack (1922) Harold (1924) and Kenneth, the baby of the family (1931), were all baptized. The Rector, Rev. Percy Stewart spelt the father's name "Kuwn Sw" when he recorded Ronald's baptism on 5 December 1920, but all the later entries in the parish registers use the more familiar spelling. The church school, St Mary's, on Meadow Lane, was also nearby and it is most likely that all the Soo children were educated there. It's highly likely too that the children grew up helping in the laundry, and they no doubt were ingrained with an ethos of hard work, but this was a family that also liked to play, and in moving to West Derby, they had moved to the right place, because the people of that area, who also liked to distinguish themselves from their Evertonian and Liverpudlian neighbours, were absolutely sports crazy.

It was, indeed, a sports crazy time. After the country had recovered from the devastating impact of the First World War, and the loss of almost an entire generation of young men, followed by the further horror of the 1919 influenza pandemic, there was a period of numb, bewildered mourning, but by the 1920s, young people wanted to move forward, and try to forget about the past, and what they wanted to do most of all was have fun. One of the greatest ways to have fun was playing sport and the Soo youngsters appear to have taken to sport like ducks to water. The residents of the West Derby area were actively and enthusiastically sporting and there were thriving cricket, tennis, rugby and hockey clubs. Cooper and Power's *History of West Derby* gives association football a central importance, however, declaring that "we dare not embark on the story of football in this area because it would need another volume to do it justice. Besides, Derbieans like Liverpudlians, imbibe the history and tradition of soccer with their mothers' milk!" In a 1975 interview with the Stoke newspaper, the *Sentinel*, Frank would echo this himself when he was asked about the attitudes of young players in the Seventies: "… some of them do not play from their hearts, as I always did. Furthermore, it was unforgiveable not to try, especially if you came from Liverpool, as I did."

Frank Soo played football for several local clubs in West Derby including the West Derby Boys' Team of 1929. A photograph of that team shows a young Frank, with his trademark smile – which can only be described as "beaming" - sitting in the middle row. Interestingly, a Hong Kong newspaper published a short item about him in 1938 which said that Frank's nickname at Stoke City was '"Smiler." Standing behind him was Jack Balmer, who was a little younger than Frank and would go on to play as a striker for Liverpool FC between 1935 and 1952, making 289 appearances and scoring ninety-eight goals. Frank is also pictured, in the same characteristic pose, in a photograph of the West Derby Boys' Club team of 1930/31, and another of the West Derby football team in 1930. Several newspaper reports written in the early stages of Frank's football career refer to him playing for Liverpool schoolboys as well. In later life, Joe Mercer, another great footballer, remembered playing "in the same Cheshire schools' teams as Stan Cullis and Frank Soo, later international colleagues." (Obituary, *Times*, 11 August 1990). In his autobiography, *Football with a Smile*, Mercer described playing street football as a boy: "Back alley football is only a substitute for the real thing. We always had to fight for bigger and better playing fields for children. But all the same the back alleys do hold some valuable lessons of their own. For instance, playing with the small ball. If you could control a small ball with certainty, you found later that bringing down a normal ball came more easily. It was wonderful training for the eye." Frank Soo would become a superb controller of the ball, his skills undoubtedly honed in similar childhood games. It was not only Frank however. Of the seven Soo children, only the eldest, Norman, and his sister, Beattie, do not appear to have any record of playing sport at a high level. Ronnie and Kenny appear to have been talented enough to interest league football clubs. Harold and Jack also played in the lower leagues, at least for short periods. Kenny was also a talented cricketer, playing in league cricket locally. Frank appears to have excelled at every sport he tried, especially football, cricket and golf.

It seems to have been clear from early on in his sporting life that Frank was a very talented footballer, and a later item in the *Hull Daily Mail* reported that he had been watched by the scouts of several leading clubs, including representatives of both Everton and Liverpool. He played for the Liverpool side of Norwood, as well as for West Derby, and West Derby Boys' Club teams. It isn't clear why neither of the two top Liverpool clubs signed him. Later, leading local journalists and players alike would repeatedly lament that he was "allowed to escape," but escape he did. In late 1932, Bob Rogers, the secretary of Prescot Cables, a successful side in the Lancashire Combination League, which regularly played perhaps better-known teams like Morecambe and Accrington Stanley, signed the eighteen-year-old. Frank would only play for them for two months before he was offered the chance to embark upon a professional career at the highest level.

In October 1931, Frank made an appearance for New Brighton, presumably as a trialist. The team sheet for the match they played against Liverpool Cables in the Liverpool County Combination League that month listed "F. Soo" at centre half. As New Brighton were at that time in the Football League, then this match was presumably a reserve game. Nothing came of the trial and Frank never listed New Brighton as one of his former clubs.

Prescot Cables FC, a club now owned by its supporters, was then a "works" team, associated with British Insulated Callenders Cables (BICC), a major local employer in the Lancashire town of Prescot, about eight miles east of Liverpool city centre. Founded in 1884, as Prescot AFC and later known as Prescot Athletic, their association with the cable-manufacturing firm began when the company paid for a new stand for the football club. It appears that Frank also worked for what was known as "Prescot Wire Works," but it is uncertain whether he worked there for very long or in exactly what capacity. The football club had joined the Lancashire Combination League in 1927/28 and in 1929, shortly before Frank played for them, they had attempted to be elected to the Third Division of the Football League, but had failed. Despite this setback, they remained an ambitious club, bringing through, and often selling on, some exceptional footballers, such as Jimmy Holmes who would go on to play for Sheffield United and West Ham, and Bill Tunstall who transferred to Aston Villa. Match reports of the time complimented the side on its clever, attractive football and Cables must have been an entertaining team to watch, frequently scoring five or more goals in competitive matches.

According to Prescot Cables' historian, Glyn Williams, little is known about Frank's short spell as an eighteen-year-old wing-half at Hope Street, but "he made an immediate impact. In the space of a few weeks, he replaced the Cables' captain, James 'Paddy' Kane and attracted the attention of several leading football clubs." Frank quickly endeared himself to the Prescot faithful by scoring two goals in a match that ended in the 5-4 defeat of Cables reserves by league leaders Calderstones on 5 November 1932. It sounds like a lively encounter featuring four penalties. Prescot Cables were a strong, high-scoring side that made great use of its wingers. In late December 1932, they beat Bacup Borough 10-0, and although Frank was not on the list of goal scorers or mentioned in the brief newspaper reports of that particular match, he obviously made a contribution to Cables' success during the very brief time that he was there. He also made a positive impression on several scouts from Football League clubs who became interested in signing him as a professional player. It was at this time that the Stoke City team was in Lancashire playing Stockport

County in the Central League and it was perhaps on this occasion that the ambitious Stoke manager, Tom Mather, decided to take a look at some up-and-coming footballers in the area. One of the players he was interested in was Frank Soo.

Little is known about Frank's brief time at Cables, although journalist Hyder Jawád interviewed a player called Jack Roscoe who was at the club at the same time and remembered him as being "clearly ahead of his time." Prescot Cables were in a four-way tussle for the top place in the Lancashire Combination League, vying with Chorley, Darwen and Fleetwood for the top spot and they may have felt that, with prolific goal scorers like Jack Roscoe on their books, they could afford to let a promising, but unproven, young player like Frank go. Frank was in the first team for a New Year's match in poor weather conditions – "wind and driving rain" – in which Cables defeated Morecambe by five goals to two. In front of a crowd of 500 spectators, on 2 January 1933, they gave Morecambe "a lesson in tactics," according to the *Lancashire Evening Post*. Even when they lost, the main criticism the local press made of Cables was that they tried to play "tricky football" which was not always suited to the conditions. According to a club history of Prescot Cables, *From Slacky Brow to Hope Street*, written by Neville Walker, "Frank became an instant hit with the Hope Street fans. Stoke soon declared an interest in the lad and paid around £400 for his signature." Soo had been playing as a wing-half for Prescot, but would convert to inside-left when he joined the Stoke City side, a squad that would include within its ranks such well-known players as Bob McGrory, Arthur Tutin, and another promising and talented young winger, a local lad called Stanley Matthews.

2

'A WORKING CLASS HERO IS SOMETHING TO BE'
Stoke-on-Trent, 1933 - 1939

When Tom Mather brought Frank Soo down to Stoke City in January 1933, the eighteen-year-old was just one of a number of adroit signings that the ambitious manager had made since his arrival at the club ten years earlier. Mather was a very different figure from the kind of football club manager that we would recognize today. In the years before the Second World War, a professional football club was usually run by what was known as a secretary-manager, a dark-suited, and often bowler-hatted, official who would do everything from drawing up contracts with players to - at some clubs - buying the stationery. Secretary-managers like Scott Duncan, of Manchester United and Ipswich Town, and Herbert Chapman at Arsenal, ran clubs as if they were factory offices or insurance firms, leaving most of the sporting activities and coaching to other staff. Although he did some coaching, Mather, who had never played football at a high level, if at all, seems to have been quite typical of the managers of his time and could most accurately be described as a professional administrator.

Tom Mather had performed a similar role at Bolton Wanderers before the First World War, returning to football as secretary-manager of Southend United in 1920 after serving in the Royal Navy. Stoke City historian, Simon Lowe, describes Mather as having a "genial persona [which] endeared him to supporters. The chirpy Lancastrian, never seen without his trademark bowler hat, wing collar and tie, stood only 5ft. 5in. and was towered over by almost the entire team. Often seen patrolling the environs of the Victoria Ground with his cane, supervising training, his strength lay in identifying players' best positions."

In 1923, the then Stoke City manager, Jock Rutherford, had walked out of the club after only four months in the job, and Mather had taken his place. Stoke City had been relegated from the First Division at the end of the 1922/23 season and relations between the club and its players were not good. Mather managed to turn things around to an extent and Stoke finished the next season in sixth place, but life at the Victoria Ground was not always very easy for the new manager. In 1923/24, a group of aggrieved players, who had either not been offered new contracts or had been asked to accept a wage reduction, turned up at the Stoke City ground in a taxi and smashed up the offices and dressing rooms. They had caused a great deal of damage before they were stopped. Mather knew that he would have to work hard to impose his authority on such a squad and he quickly made some significant changes, including transferring some fans' favourites, such as Jimmy Broad, Joe Kasher and Billy Tempest, out to other clubs. His strategy did not pay off at first, and Stoke's fortunes failed to improve. They finished in twentieth place at the end of the 1924/25 campaign, and the following season they were relegated to the Third Division (North) for the first time in the club's history.

The club kept faith with Mather, however, and there followed a decade of stability at the Victoria Ground when the club had the same chairman, (A. J. C. Sherwin, 1924-36), manager (Mather, 1923-35), and captain (McGrory, 1925-35), followed by Bob McGrory taking over as manager from 1935 until 1952. This consistency appears to have had a hugely positive effect on Stoke as a club, and it went on to have a period of success during the 1930s which City - one of the founder members of the Football League - had not witnessed before and arguably would never see again. Mather was not to be deterred by the club's decline and carried on rebuilding his team, bringing in players from all around the country, including Bobby Archibald, a left-winger from Third Lanark, full-back Billy Spencer from Hebden Bridge and Charlie Wilson from Huddersfield Town. The club's board, especially its chairman, A. J. C. Sherwin, shared Mather's ambitions and in 1928, secured the ownership of the freehold on the Victoria Ground, which would continue to be Stoke City's home until the move to the Britannia Stadium (currently known as the bet365 Stadium) in 1997. The 1929/30 season saw the opening of a new covered section of the Butler Street stand, increasing the ground's capacity by 12,000. The total capacity of the Victoria Ground had reached 50,000 spectators (some say as many as 70,000) and the revenues from these bigger crowds would be vital in bringing in the income to back Stoke City's ambitions in the Football League.

Tom Mather appears to have been very astute in the selection of players that he brought in during the early 1930s, although he did have the immense good fortune that Stanley Matthews, the talented son of a local barber and amateur boxer, was living just down the road, and having brought him in as a fifteen-year-old apprentice, Mather signed Matthews on professional terms on his seventeenth birthday in February 1932. In his autobiography, *The Way It Was*, Matthews remembered that the manager was absolutely determined to obtain his signature, recalling that "Stoke City manager Tom Mather must have had the best groomed hair in Stoke-on-Trent. Following my successful debut for England schoolboys, he called into my father's barber's shop every day. Father would sit him down and say, 'The usual?'" So concerned was Mather that another club might come in and steal his footballing prodigy that, according to Matthews, he posted men on the main roads in and out of Stoke-on-Trent to check the number plates of cars coming into the city in case they were from a rival club that might poach his young star from under his nose. If nothing else, this story illustrates Mather's single-mindedness and ruthless determination. If he was anything like as adamant about signing Frank Soo, it is easy to understand why he was able to beat clubs like Liverpool and Everton and bring the young Liverpudlian player to Stoke-on-Trent. The signing made the pages of the *Daily Mirror* on 26 January 1933: "Stoke City yesterday signed on Frank Soo, the Chinese footballer who has latterly been watched by Everton, Liverpool, Aston Villa, and other famous clubs," and the *Hull Daily Mail* added to a similar report that "Soo is nicely built, smart, and plays right half." Even the *Straits Times*, an English-language newspaper in Singapore, carried the news of Frank's move to Stoke, managing to be effusive and insulting at the same time:

FRANK SOO. FIRST CHINESE TO PLAY IN ENGLISH LEAGUE

Frank Soo, Stoke City's Chinese footballer, is the most romantic personality in the Potteries at the moment. He is the first and only Chinese footballer to play in the English league football. Frank is 19. Oriental looking, but handsome. He has a flashing, dazzling smile, a modest demeanour; and a thoroughly English accent. ...

The crowd admire him for his sunny disposition and for his cleverness as a footballer.

'I am very glad to have realised my ambition to play for a First Division club – but let us talk about something else,' he says.

He is a player of above the average intelligence, with a deceptive swerve, amazingly clever ball control, and a deadly shot with both feet. He should go far. Frank is popular not only with the spectators at Stoke but with all his fellow professionals, not one of whom has failed to congratulate him on his promotion to the League team, and wish him luck.

His hobby is his work – football. His vice – golf.

Even at the age of nineteen, Frank sounds as if he was more amused than overwhelmed by the attention he was receiving and the article, although fulsome, is more open in its racial attitudes with its sly, gratuitous insult masquerading as a compliment, than the British press. The *Singapore Free Press* also ran a brief news item about the signing, and had managed to get a rare quote from the Stoke City coach (and soon to be father-in-law of Stanley Matthews), Jimmy Vallance who told them "Soo is a little wonder with any kind of ball. He is always thinking out tricks, and often gets away with tactics which leave other teams completely puzzled." Crowds, according to this newspaper loved him, and they had already given him the nickname "Smiler." It's not difficult to see why.

Mather (and his successor, Bob McGrory) ran a rather paternalistic regime at the Victoria Ground. Players were all given a list of regulations about their behaviour, which included only being allowed to drink on special occasions, and when the team took a train to away matches they were marched from the railway station to the opposition's ground in pairs like a crocodile of schoolboys. Tales of rebellion were rife. When the team was playing away from home, Jimmy Vallance would keep watch on the doors of the players' hotel bedrooms in an effort to stop them from smuggling alcohol in. On one occasion, several players ended up sleeping on the floor of the teetotal Matthews' bedroom after sneaking in some booze, which they then drank communally out of a chamber pot. It's unlikely that Frank would have been involved in such japes as he was committed to his fitness, and as abstemious as Matthews was.

Stoke City had been promoted back to the second division of the Football League at the end of the 1926/27 season and it did not take long before they were challenging for a return to the top flight. They had to wait until the end of the 1932/33 season before they finally achieved promotion and went back to the First Division as champions having accrued fifty-six points from forty-two games, beating Tottenham Hotspur to the top spot by one point. Mather's ambitions for the club are obvious looking at the kind of players that he brought in during this period, such as Arthur Tutin (from Aldershot), Arthur Turner (West Bromwich Albion) and George Antonio (Oswestry Town). He wanted strong, reliable players, who were capable of winning the ball and who would get the ball to his fast and tricky wingers, most notably Matthews. Match reports in newspapers of this time describe Stoke City as being one of the most exciting and attractive sides in the Football League, playing in a style that used the skills of footballers like Stanley Matthews and Frank Soo to great effect. A report in the *Evening Sentinel*, on 28 January 1938, of a match against Bradford, is typical: "Stoke began to give football lessons - a wonderful flick by Soo, some dazzling footwork by Antonio, a bit of trickery from Tutin, and, of course, some samples of Matthews' wizardry... ." Such descriptions of the Stoke City side were not uncommon in this era - even by the supporters of rival clubs - and even when they failed to defeat their opponents, commentators were full of admiration for the excitement and beauty of their style of play.

During Mather's time at Stoke, full-back Bob McGrory became the key player in the side. He was a tough, uncompromising Scot - on and off the pitch, by all accounts - who had come to the club in 1921 after a difficult period at Burnley. He took on the role of second team player-coach during the 1932/33 season, and was clearly intended to become Mather's eventual successor as manager. McGrory was coming to the end of a long playing career when Frank arrived at the Victoria Ground, but he was still sometimes recalled to the first team when it was necessary, and he was still playing occasionally for the Stoke first team in 1935 at the age of 44. Frank was already impressing coaches and supporters alike with his elegance and exciting skills when playing for the reserves. As the reserves' coach, McGrory had a great deal to do with the younger players and new recruits like Frank Soo. It seems as if he played a major part in bringing Frank through to become a regular member of the first team. Although there were some clear difficulties between the two towards the end of Soo's career at Stoke, it should be remembered that it was McGrory who gave Frank most of his opportunities as a first-team player, and who would eventually appoint him as team captain.

The city of Stoke-on-Trent to which Frank Soo moved in 1933 would not have been very different from the urban areas where he had grown up in Sheffield and Liverpool, although Stoke's primary industry was pottery manufacture which meant that distinctive bottle-shaped kilns were scattered across the city's skyline. Other industries, such as coal mining and engineering had created an ugly environment of sprawling streets, tiny terraced houses, factories, municipal buildings and pitheads. Industrial and domestic pollution had created a pall of thick smoke, which hung permanently over the city leaving what had originally been red-stone and brick buildings completely black in colour. The conurbation was not just made up of Five Towns, the term coined to describe the Potteries by the locally-born novelist Arnold Bennett in 1902, but a sprawling network of canals, railway lines and industrial villages. Some, like Etruria, the home of Wedgwood, were entirely based around one factory. After J. B. Priestley visited Stoke when he was writing his *English Journey*, which was published in 1934, not long after Frank's arrival there, he described it as "grim, smoky, dingy, dirty, shabby, preposterous... and extremely ugly." He went on: "I have seen few regions from which Nature has been banished more ruthlessly, and banished only in favour of a sort of troglodyte mankind. Civilized man, except in his capacity as a working potter, has not arrived here yet... . Their excellent services of buses... simply take you from one absence of civic dignity to another... these differences are minute when compared with the awful gap between the whole lot of them and any civilized urban region." Scathing as it was, Priestley's impression was also quite superficial and ignored the fact that the Potteries were set in an area of distinctive rural beauty, close to the Staffordshire moorlands and the Peak District. Passing through, Priestley would not have had the time to learn of the warmth, kindness and humour of the people there, the toughness of whose lives was mitigated somewhat by an extremely strong sense of community and social solidarity, including a deep and abiding passion for its famous football club. Frank Soo certainly appears to have found the area a perfectly acceptable one in which to live. Returning to the city in 1975, after he had been living in Sweden for many years, he told the local newspaper that he had loved his time at Stoke and had "never wanted to leave." He had a strong affection for local people in particular, recalling: "The Potteries folk were marvellous to me and the ground was nearly always full when we played." In the same interview, he recalled that his starting wage at Stoke City had been fifty shillings a week.

Stoke had a very small Chinese community at this time, mainly made up of Chinese-run laundries as was the case elsewhere. There were nineteen such businesses in the Stoke area according to the 1932 Kelly's Post Office Directory, but it doesn't appear that Frank had very much connection - if any - with other Chinese people in the Potteries, despite the constant references to his ethnicity in the press. Frank's life in Stoke-on-Trent seems to have been much the same as that of any other young professional footballer. He trained, played football, made appearances at charity events, and found time for his other great passion, golf. It has been said that he also worked in a laundry under the Boothen End of the Victoria Ground when he was a young player. It is impossible to find any evidence of this, but it seems possible, given his background and the fact that most footballers had to take on other jobs just to survive, as wages were so low at this time. Generally, professional footballers were not paid, or were paid less, in the close season too, so they had to find work over the summer break. Housing arrangements could also be very basic, particularly for the younger, unmarried players. Most young players, unless they were local boys like Matthews, lived in lodgings or "digs," and Frank probably did so too. For example, the electoral register for Stoke-on-Trent shows that he was living in the city centre, at 102 Richmond Street, Penkhull, the home of Annie and Freddie Platt, for at least three years until the time of his wedding in 1938.

As young men of the same age - the future "wizard of the dribble" was born just under a year after Soo - Frank and Stan Matthews would often find their career paths intertwining, and they would not only play together at Stoke City for many years, but would later both be picked to play for England in several Wartime and Victory internationals, although Matthews of course won many more official England caps than Frank. In the early days, according to one source, they also acted as linesmen, running the line together at the same games such as local charity fundraising matches. Despite being the younger of the two, Matthews was certainly the better established at the club. He was local - he had been born and brought up in one of the Five Towns, Hanley - and had been at the club, mainly polishing boots and running errands, since he was fifteen years old. Oddly, although they played together at Stoke from 1933 until 1939, Matthews barely mentions Frank in any of his five books of memoirs. In fact, he doesn't refer to him at all when writing about his time at the Potteries' club. The only references that Matthews does make are in anecdotes about incidents that occurred when they were on international duty together. This seems a little strange as they both played for Stoke so often, although when Matthews does refer to Frank, the tone is friendly. He always calls him Frankie, as most people did, and refers to him as a fellow "Stokie." Whether the omission from his memoirs was made through professional rivalry, and there's no evidence to suggest that it was, or simply because they were so familiar to one another that Matthews took Frank's presence for granted, it's difficult to tell, but it is distinctly odd that Matthews didn't write about his friend more.

What we can find out about Frank's time at Stoke City has to be gleaned from match reports and comments about him by the sports writers of the day. Many of those comments referred to Frank as "the Chinese player," particularly in the early days. His debut for the Stoke City first team warranted a whole column in the *Daily Express* of 1 November 1933, illustrated by a portrait of the young star ("who is 5 ft. 7½ ins, and weighs 10 st. 2 lbs.," according to another report in the *Evening Telegraph* of the same date):

SOO GETS HIS CHANCE IN SENIOR FOOTBALL: CHINESE TO PLAY IN STOKE ATTACK

Stoke City will complete today the transfer of Arthur Tutin, right half-back, of Aldershot. Tutin is to play on Saturday in the side to meet Middlesbrough.

Frank Soo, the Chinese forward who has been appearing with Stoke City Reserves, will also turn out for the first eleven.

He will appear at inside left in place of Davies, who has been moved to inside right, Ware being excluded. ... Frank Soo is the first and only Chinese to play in English league football, and when he steps on to the field at Middlesbrough he will realise one of the ambitions of his life.

Soo joined Stoke City about eighteen months ago from Prescot Cables. His father is the owner of a Chinese laundry in Liverpool, and young Soo, before taking up football as a career with Stoke, was employed at the cable works at Prescot.

He is a brilliant player and the idol of the crowd at Stoke, as well as being popular with his colleagues. He has played consistently in the Stoke Central League team, and his artistry and power of marksmanship have attracted attention all over the country.

Soo was born at Buxton, but when a baby his parents moved to Liverpool where he lived until he joined Stoke. He has never been out of England. His great hobby is golf, and he plays regularly on midland golf courses.

Stoke City made a flying start to the 1933/34 season but began to fall away, which may be the reason why Mather decided to give Frank his debut in the first team. He had already become the darling of those Potters' fans who had seen him play for the reserves. Many newspapers, including the national titles, singled him out for particular attention, partly because they saw some novelty in having a "Chinese" footballer in a prominent side, but also undoubtedly because he showed such great promise and flair as a player. His highly anticipated debut didn't work out so well, however, as City went down to a heavy defeat at Middlesbrough. The Stoke-on-Trent local newspaper, the *Sentinel*, reported: "The surprise about Stoke's reverse was that they should be so soundly beaten after scoring in the first minute before any of the Middlesbrough players had even touched the ball; but after this set-back the home team showed remarkable finishing power. It was only in their shooting that they were superior to Stoke for whom Soo, the only Chinese player in football, made his debut, but it was a telling advantage." Another report told a similar story: "Stoke, who have fallen off sadly after their fine start, had six goals scored against them at Middlesbrough after taking the lead. Soo, the Chinaman, who was making his debut, was Stoke's best forward. Middlesbrough gave their best display of the season." The reference to Soo as a "Chinaman" was typical of this period in his career. On occasions, writers such as this one in the *Western Daily Press*, would use his origins as an excuse to indulge themselves in a cavalcade of clichés: "At Middlesbrough, Stoke City went off with a bang, scoring in the first minute, but the home side played inspired football after this reverse, and netted six times. Frank Soo, Stoke's Chinese debutant, proved a real 'cracker.'"

Stoke's next game was on 11 November 1933 against Manchester City at the Victoria Ground and although they were not thrashed as they had been at Ayresome Park, they still lost by a goal to nil. Frank continued to receive attention from the press all over the country including this short piece in the *Yorkshire Evening Post* entitled "The Chinaman":

> A noticeable newcomer to Association first league football is a young Chinaman of the name of Soo. He made his debut in the league game at Middlesbrough on Saturday last in the match which the Boro' played with Stoke City. Reports credit him with having played well in the Stoke forward line.
>
> Yet it should be nothing surprising to find a Chinaman playing football. 'Old Timer,' of Ilkley, in an appreciation which he has written of the book by Phe Der Chen, notes that author's claim that China played football five thousand years ago. I am unable of my own knowledge to dispute the claim, but I'm inclined to regard it as a bit of leg pulling.

The existence of a game that was very similar to football in Han Dynasty China (206 BCE - 220 CE) would probably not have been known to the author of this particular piece of sarcasm, and it's likely that, if he had known, he would not have believed that the origins of association football lay anywhere other than on the playing fields of an English boys' school.

Frank's Chinese background certainly attracted the attention of both local and national newspapers, but he was also noticed because of his undoubted talent. Stanley Warren, in the *Daily Express*, 18 November 1933, wrote, in a preview of the weekend's matches, including Stoke versus Arsenal, "Highbury supporters will not see John the goalkeeper who helped Wales to retain the international title. Stoke prefer Lewis. But they will see Frank Soo, the young Chinese inside left, who will be playing his third game in First Division football" and on 29 December, his name appeared on the back page of the *Daily Mirror*: "It is unlikely that Chelsea spectators will see Frank Soo, Stoke's Chinese player, in action. He is very young, and Mr. Mather's idea is to give him only an occasional run with the Potter's league team until he has gained greater experience with the reserves. He is really [a] left half but it was as an inside left that he was chosen when they visited Highbury last month. At present he is called on only in the event of Sellars or Sale being unfit."

Frank had to wait until December to win his first match, as Stoke again lost at Highbury against Arsenal (3-0) on 18 November in front of 38,000 spectators. He was dropped for the next six games, only returning to the first team for the home fixture against Leicester City on Christmas Day and the return away match against the same side on Boxing Day. His exclusion does not appear to have made a great deal of difference to the team's fortunes as they only won one game in his absence, a two-nil victory over Blackburn Rovers at the Victoria Ground on 9 December 1933. On his return, Stoke lost again, this time away at Stamford Bridge but the side's form soon picked up and Stoke won four out of their five matches in January 1934. The Potters were now in a triangular relegation battle with Chelsea and Sheffield United at the foot of Division One.

By the end of January 1934, there was talk of a "Stoke revival," with the *Dundee Courier* reporting on their home match against Huddersfield Town on the 29th: "Stoke outclassing their opponents and winning as easily as the score [3-0] suggests. The Stoke forwards ran into their best form, and Soo and [Tommy] Sale each scored within the first two minutes of the resumption. Matthews, the outstanding attacker, and [Joe] Johnson had splendid shots saved by Turner before the first-named scored a third goal six minutes from time." This was Frank's first league goal for Stoke – he had also scored a goal in each of the FA Cup ties against Bradford Park Avenue and Blackpool but they were to be his only first team goals of the season. Never prolific, Frank would only score nineteen goals in 326 Football League appearances for his many clubs. He was still much admired because of the number of goals that he helped to create. Besides, City hardly needed many goals from Soo. By the end of the 1933/34 season they had scored 129 goals in total, seven more than the league champions, Arsenal. Despite this, Stoke's season continued to be indifferent, although they finished in a respectable twelfth place with forty-one points.

Stoke began the 1934/35 season strongly with an 8-1 thrashing of Leeds United at home and a 2-0 win against Birmingham, but Frank didn't feature until the away match against Leeds on 3 September. There was clearly stiff competition for places on the wing at Stoke City. Six of the eight goals scored against Leeds were scored by wingers, Matthews (4), and Johnson (2), while the other two had been picked up by Stoke's prolific centre forward, Tommy Sale. Frank only played eight matches in the first team during this season and did not score for them at all, but he still impressed the dedicated fans who watched Stoke City reserves. A typical, perhaps claret-tinted, match report, in the Lancashire-based *Express and News*, described a reserves game in which he scored a hat-trick:

SIX GOALS CONCEDED
RESERVES FIND STOKE TOO GOOD FOR THEM

Stoke City Reserves 6 Burnley Reserves 2

Curtis and Soo (2) scored for the visitors before the interval. On the resumption Robson increased Stoke's score and later Soo completed his hat-trick. Cecil Smith reduced the arrears, but Robson again found the net for the visitors. Before the end, Hornby scored a second goal for Burnley.

Stoke City reserves have scored 41 goals and their opponents 14. At Burnley they fully justified their claim to such a wonderful goal average. On this day's showing they would beat many a Second Division team. They showed splendid method, their forwards, led by an opportunist leader in Robson, were crafty and enterprising, while their defence was steady as the proverbial rock. They fully deserved to take both points away from Turf Moor.

At the same time the score at half-time flattered them. They were entitled to lead perhaps but they were certainly not three goals better than Burnley; unfortunately slips by the home defence helped them. Scott did not seem far off stopping Curtis's shot which sent the ball into the net almost at crawling speed. Soo's first goal was also a simple one. His second he back-heeled into the net from a rather remarkable angle. Many people alleged he handled it. ... Later the Stoke centre-forward got clean through again in a breakaway and then slipped the ball across to Soo, who completed his 'hat-trick.'

Soo did, however, play for the first team in the defeat of close rivals Derby County at the Baseball Ground on 8 September 1934. The *Derby Evening Telegraph* correspondent rather begrudgingly allowed that his team had been outplayed, but he also painted an interesting picture of how well the Stoke team were playing at that time: "I was particularly impressed with the right-wing trio, Tutin, (Bobby) Liddle and Matthews. They combined brilliantly, and they were largely responsible for (Eric) Keen having a poor match. Soo, at inside-left, proved almost as fine a tactician as Liddle, and it was at inside that Stoke had a tremendous advantage. The Stoke men, without holding up the progress of the line, worked the ball cleverly and drew the opposition before making judicious passes to the wingers... in the tenth minute, Stoke gave the home forwards an object lesson in quick, crisp football. Following an advance on the right, the ball was promptly switched into the middle, and though a Derby defender might have got it away, Soo was quick to take advantage of the opening and heading the ball straight down to Sale... the centre-forward, without a moment's hesitation, flashed the ball past Kirby." Stoke won the match by two goals to nil. By 27 October 1934, after twelve games, Stoke City had become leaders of the First Division for the first time in their history.

Frank was not selected to play in the sixth round of the FA Cup that season, which was against Manchester City at Maine Road. The match attracted a crowd of 84,569, a record attendance that stood for years. In fact, Soo was dropped from the first team for a long time and didn't play for them again between the end of September 1934 and 9 March 1935 when he was recalled after Stoke had lost three games in a row. He returned to another home defeat against Chelsea but quickly made a good impression upon observers. A reporter at Stoke's next match at Roker Park on 16 March 1935 found little that was praiseworthy about Sunderland's opponents – who were defeated by four goals to one, apart from "Soo [who] was by far the best in the Stoke side in trying to develop attack, but with twenty-five minutes of the game gone Thorpe [the Sunderland goalkeeper] had only once had to handle the ball. Soo made another capital attempt to get through by hooking the ball over Murray's head, but he had to get on to one knee to deliver a shot and he sent it square across the goal where Johnson's foot did the necessary. ... Stoke got their first corner of the match when after clever collaboration between Johnson and Soo, the outside left's shot was intercepted by Sunderland's centre half and turned for a corner."

Frank played his next first team game against Everton on 31 March 1935. It was another defeat, this time by five goals to nil. His next appearance was in a Stoke City XI that played in a benefit match for Bristol City's half-back, Ernie Brinton, at Ashton Gate. The *Western Daily Press* singled Soo out in its headline as the "star":

> Stoke, who fielded a strong team, owed their success to their superior stamina and relentless fighting until the final whistle went. They were the more scientific XI, and their methodical play was pretty to watch.
>   A lot of interest was naturally centred around three of their men – Scattergood and Johnson, two ex-Bristol City players, and Soo, who is of Chinese descent. This sleek-haired inside-right was a fine dribbler, and his habit of tricking the Bristol men by throwing the ball up behind to a teammate as he was on the move often confused the home defence. ... The pace of the game livened up considerably in the second half. When Stoke made a determined attempt to reduce Bristol's lead. Soo demonstrated his remarkable ball control and was unlucky not to score in the first attempt. His quick but calculated mastery of the ball was again seen immediately afterwards when he sent a ball into the net from a corner almost before Dolman realised what had happened.

Soo was named on the list of retained players issued by Stoke City at the end of the 1934/35 season. Six others were transfer listed. After the season was over City went on a short tour of Denmark. They won all of the three games they played there quite comfortably, including matches against a Copenhagen XI and a Danish select XI. This may have been Frank's introduction to Scandinavia, a part of the world he would return to many times and it was also where he was to eventually settle there and spend many years working as a coach and club manager after he retired from playing football. However, around this time, Soo broke his leg and it's possible that he missed the tour altogether, although he may have accompanied his teammates to Denmark even if he did not play. He certainly only officially returned from the injury in the match against Liverpool at Anfield on 18 September 1935. The new season would see him playing regularly and he became a vital part of the side under the new manager, Bob McGrory, who took over the job from Tom Mather when the latter became the manager of Newcastle United in June 1935.

   When Mather left for Newcastle United he left the Potteries' club in a very strong position, both financially and in terms of the potential of the squad that he had built. It was never made clear why Mather left when he did. It was initially suggested that he would continue just as club secretary with McGrory taking over the manager's side of the job, but after an offer came for his services from Newcastle United, Mather left, expressing his wish that he could have remained at the Victoria Ground: "I'm glad I'm leaving it a better club than I found it," he said, sounding somewhat disappointed.

It was Bob McGrory who reaped most of the benefit of Mather's work, however, although it's thought that Mather made an unsuccessful attempt to take both Stanley Matthews and Frank Soo with him to the north east. On 1 August 1935 the *Portsmouth Evening News* reported that "Frank Soo, Stoke's Chinese player, has been discussed in the Newcastle United boardrooms." If it were true that Tom Mather intended to take his best players with him to Tyneside, he had miscalculated the tenacity of McGrory, the man he had groomed as his own successor for many years. As Stoke City historian, Simon Lowe writes of him: "If 'dour' described McGrory's approach on the field, it aptly summed up the bluff Scot's personality off it." His toughness, both in character and physically, stood him in good stead, and much of his career had been free from injury, enabling him to take over the captaincy from Milne in 1925, a role which he performed for ten years, making him Stoke City's longest-serving captain. McGrory was a very different personality from the easy-going Mather, and some people regarded him as "abrasive." The *Yorkshire Evening Post* described McGrory's approach to youth team coaching: "In private practice matches at the Victoria Ground, McGrory, the Stoke City right back, sometimes plays as inside forward, so that he can be 'bang on the premises,' so to speak, to inculcate the proper tactical ideas in the young bloods."

The broken leg kept Frank on the sidelines between March 1935 and the beginning of the 1935/36 season and he missed Stoke's 3-0 drubbing of Chelsea on 10 September. His return to the first team at Anfield on the 18th saw Stoke lose, but his second match after coming back into the side was a huge victory when the team beat Birmingham by five goals to nil on 21 September 1935. McGrory introduced Frank back into this new, more defensive position very gradually by playing him in the reserves. Soo had been playing as an inside left under Mather but was now being asked to perform the role of a left-sided half-back. In September 1935, Stoke City stalwart Harry Sellars, who had been first choice in that position for many years, injured his knee badly. He was coming to the end of a long career at Stoke, having made more than 350 appearances in league football for them. Sellars' injury was a blow to the side, but it enabled McGrory to begin building what would become one of Stoke's great half-back lines of Tutin, Turner and Soo. Soo's tactical awareness and his almost magical ball-playing skills combined perfectly with the gritty, hard-working Tutin and Turner. Frank quickly made the position his own. The move appears to have suited him and, although he scored no goals that season, he became an established part of a defensive partnership that would stand his team in good stead for many years to come. Later, in his autobiography, *Football is my Game*, Stan Mortensen picked Frank Soo out as one of the four finest wing-halves that he had ever played with, adding that "as a feeder of forwards, he was perhaps neater than the other three [George Farrow, Billy Wright and Joe Mercer], but perhaps not quite so destructive when it came to breaking up the other side's moves. Everything he did was hall-marked, however, and he seemed incapable of a clumsy movement."

Frank rarely put a foot wrong, and the Stoke scouts kept returning to Prescot Cables to look for more hidden talent. They signed John Almond from Cables in 1934, but he was not a success, moving on to Tranmere Rovers in 1936 after making only three first-team appearances and scoring a single goal.

From this time on, Frank became the object of great admiration, not just in the Potteries but nationwide. The Arsenal and Scotland international, Alex James, described Frank as "modern for his time." Although results were still mixed - Stoke lost 0-3 to both Grimsby Town and Sheffield Wednesday - this was a period of consolidation for the side and they finished the 1935/36 season in fourth place in Division One - Stoke City's highest ever finishing position - having also had a good run in the FA Cup, only going out in a fifth round replay defeat at Barnsley. Frank played thirty-six games for the Stoke first team in the 1935/36 season, but didn't score. Despite this, he was winning praise from everyone who saw him play, and calls for him to be selected for England were becoming louder. A match preview in the *Derby Evening Telegraph* on 13 March 1936, described him thus: "A dandy little player of subtle touch and classic style, he failed to score in twenty games in his original position, but since his conversion in September, international honours have been predicted for him." McGrory is remembered as one of Stoke's best ever managers and it was under his direction that the first team developed into one of the best sides in the country, including a consistent defence, made up of Norman Wilkinson, Bill Winstanley, Charles Scrimshaw, Arthur Tutin, Arthur Turner and Soo, which played thirty successive games between December 1935 and September 1936. The half-back line with Tutin and Turner which, according to Martin Wade in his club history, *A Potter's Tale,* "Many current supporters, whose memories go back that far, still consider the best Stoke ever had and, as a line, they played together eighty-five times." Unfortunately, McGrory's personality was not always conducive to good relations with the players. He most famously fell out with Stanley Matthews, other players recalling them "going at it hammer and tongs" in the manager's office. Frank too, would eventually fall victim to what has been described as McGrory's "pathological dislike of star players."

Not everyone was impressed by Soo, as this report from a Derby newspaper of a match between Stoke City and Derby County at the Baseball Ground on 14 March 1936 shows: "They [Derby] rarely failed to get the ball across, particularly Crooks, who made it apparent from the start that he could beat Soo and Scrimshaw. The latter certainly kicked well, but that was all, and both he and Soo were spoken to by the referee for their unfair methods against England's best right winger. ... I was rather disappointed with Soo and Tutin. I have seen the two wing-halves play some glorious games, but on Saturday they were only seen to advantage in an attacking role. ... Soo never got the measure of Crooks, and though he worked well in attack, he frequently caused his side anxiety by his inability to check the Derby winger."

Stanley Matthews first had a disagreement with McGrory after loyalty bonuses were awarded to some players at the end of the 1935/36 season. The club had made a record profit of £8,420 and was able to issue a dividend to shareholders. The bonus payments were £500 for five years' service and £650 for players who had been with the club for longer. Matthews felt that his time as an apprentice, which would have earned him the larger sum, should have been taken into account. The row rumbled on for some time until the manager referred the matter to the Stoke City board which effectively put any decision off until the following summer when the directors at first came down in McGrory's favour. Matthews, aware that his presence in the team was vital to Stoke's financial and footballing success, dug in his heels and reluctantly the board backed down and paid him the higher bonus. It is interesting to see how similar Matthews and Soo were in this regard. Towards the end of his time at the Victoria Ground, Frank would also have run-ins with the Stoke board about wages and would not be afraid of standing up for what he believed to be right at his other clubs later on in his career. In the era of the maximum wage when many players had to take on labouring jobs or other work during the summer recess in order to make ends meet, these battles over points of principle were important. In fact, it's likely that Soo was vocal in the Matthews dispute. For many years, he was the player to whom journalists turned most often when there was any problem over professional footballers' wages or contracts. He does not appear in any histories of the Players' Union, as the predecessor of the Professional Footballers' Association (PFA) was known, and he seems not to have had a formal role, but over the years, Frank Soo became a regular spokesman for many players in their battle to improve their lot.

Soo again played a great deal of football in the 1936/37 season and continued to draw the admiration of many commentators. According to the *Daily Worker*, who seemed to have taken a shine to Frank, he was training hard in an effort to get back into the first team: "Reports indicate that he will be fit and ready if wanted by Stoke for the first match." Stoke began the new season with a defeat at Liverpool but Soo's performance in an away match at Charlton Athletic was singled out for praise in syndicated match reports. By the end of September, commentators were beginning to notice just how good this Stoke team were, as the *Portsmouth Evening News* reported: "Stoke City are running into brilliant form, but their 6-2 thrashing of Middlesbrough was not quite expected." Other sports writers predicted that they could even be champions. This was to be a season when the Potters were to mete out some humiliating defeats. In addition to the result against Boro', they beat Birmingham City 4-2 and, on 4 February 1937, in a remarkable match, they defeated West Bromwich Albion by ten goals to three. They also beat Sunderland 5-3 in March 1937 and Brentford 5-1 in the penultimate game of the season. Stoke were inconsistent, especially away from home, and injuries to key players like Steele and Liddle took their toll. They finished the season in a disappointing tenth place, which was particularly frustrating because they were playing some of the best, most stylish football in the club's history and had been tipped for a much higher position towards the top of the championship.

One of the reasons for the team's improvement was that another forward, the Hanley-born youngster Freddie Steele, had come into great form. He would be picked for England six times that season, and score eight international goals mainly in the home internationals. Stoke's play would be all about getting the ball through to Steele who scored thirty-three club goals in the season, including five hat-tricks and one five-goal haul in the West Bromwich Albion game. Unfortunately, Soo was to miss that match, and the whole of January and February 1937 through another injury, only returning to the first team for the away match at Old Trafford on 6 March, although he did feature in the heavy defeats of Sunderland and Brentford. In November 1937, Stoke were so badly affected by player injuries, that McGrory held "secret trials" behind closed doors, where he tried players out in various positions, including Frank Soo as a centre forward. The three regular Stoke centre forwards, Steele, Westland and Massey were all out. Despite the enthusiasm of several local newspaper reporters for the experiment, Frank only played twice in this position before reverting to half-back. In December, he was switched again, this time back to his old attacking midfield position and, although he spent almost all of the second half of the season there, he was at inside left again for the final two games in May 1938. The injury crisis, and McGrory's efforts to address it, did not go down well with supporters, however and, following an FA Cup replay, in which Stoke lost 2-1 to Bradford Park Avenue of the Second Division, the *Daily Express* reported that "Stoke spectators howled their disappointment. Five thousand surrounded the directors' box shouting, 'We want a centre forward!' About one thousand invaded the playing pitch. Situation was menacing. A hurried call brought police reinforcements, whose presence persuaded the crowd to disperse – shouting lustily. ... A two minute storm brought Stoke a goal through Frank Soo." Injuries, including yet another to Soo, had a serious effect on Stoke City's season and the club ended its twenty-fourth season in the First Division in seventeeth place with thirty-eight points.

1938 was a memorable year for Frank Soo as he was not only given the captaincy of Stoke City in March of that year, but he married his fiancée, Beryl Lunt, a 22-year-old hairdresser, who was usually known by her middle name, Freda. She was the daughter of a local art teacher, who by this time had become headmaster of the village school at Wetley Rocks in the Staffordshire moorlands. They had met after Freda, "an ardent football fan," had sent her autograph album to the Victoria Ground for the whole team to sign. Her hobby had been collecting the autographs of the theatre, musical and comedy stars who appeared at local venues such as the Regent Theatre and the Victoria Hall in Stoke-on-Trent.

At the time of her marriage to Frank, which took place at St. Peter's church in Stoke-on-Trent on 12 June 1938, she was living at "Berwyn," a neat, comfortable-looking detached bungalow in Chester Road, Audley, a village about four miles north west of Newcastle-under-Lyme. The reception was held at a café in Church Street, Audley, owned and run by Mrs May Fryer, which was known to local people as The Café. A three story building, the ground floor was a small grocer's shop with a café and function room on the first floor. May Fryer's daughter-in-law, Mrs Pat Fryer, remembers the Soos from that time, describing them as having been "very, very popular." It is perhaps a measure of the esteem in which Frank Soo was held by the people he knew at that time, that Mrs Fryer is still in possession of the white kid gloves that Frank wore that day, which he can be seen holding in his wedding photograph. News of Frank's marriage made the national press, with the *Daily Mirror* reporting the details in brief, informing its readers that the happy couple were honeymooning in Bournemouth. It was unusual for national newspapers to report anything about the private lives of professional footballers at this time and the fact that the story made the front page, is a clear indication of Frank Soo's standing as a player and a personality in the years leading up to the Second World War. Not only was the wedding reported in the British national press, it also reached the pages of the Singapore English-language newspaper, the *Straits Times*, which had been following his career since he signed for Stoke City back in 1933: "Thousands of people crowded in and around Stoke-on-Trent Parish Church to see Frank Soo, England's only footballer of Chinese extraction, and his bride, Miss Beryl Lunt... . Soo, in his four years with Stoke City - he is a half-back and one of the club's star players - has made himself one of the most popular figures in the Potteries. Leaving the church, he and his bride had to force their way through a barrage of confetti. Soo's parents, Mr and Mrs Jack Soo, - Mr Soo is Chinese, lives in Liverpool - were among the guests and their daughter, Beatrice was a bridesmaid."

Following their marriage, Frank and his wife moved to 4 Huntley Avenue, a respectable semi-detached house, in Penkhull, in the heart of the Potteries. Freda, unusually for the time, continued to work in the hairdressing salon that she owned in Church Street, Stoke. As a boy, Alan

Chadwick lived next door to them at 6 Huntley Avenue, and he remembers them well: "Freda was a really lovely woman. ... They were a lovely couple, the perfect couple, really," he says. He remembers that Frank was one of the few people in the area to own a car, "a black Austin 7," and that he was "always immaculate, sleek black hair, he had the Brylcreem look. He never had to shave. He was very softly spoken, a very nice man." Life must have been good. Frank was playing well, the calls for his selection to England were growing stronger, and he and Freda were a popular and glamorous couple, liked and admired by everyone who knew them.

The only negative aspect of Frank's life at this time was due to there being more conflict at the club, as the longstanding dispute between the directors and Stanley Matthews – rapidly turning into a saga – reached a new level in February 1938. The issues between the star and his club hit both the local and national headlines when he asked to be placed on the transfer list. According to Matthews, the problem this time arose because he had made some changes to his style of playing. Rumours had begun to circulate that an anti-Matthews clique had developed in the Stoke City dressing room, although this is something that Matthews himself denied, writing years later that "I received nothing but friendship from my Stoke teammates, but the rumours persisted and grew. Everywhere I went in Stoke people would stop and ask me how I felt about it. I kept on denying there was any truth in this story but so often was the issue brought to my attention that, being young, I did begin to wonder if in fact there may be some substance to it." Matthews felt that it was time to move on, despite the fact that he was still only twenty-three years old. When the newspaper headlines hit the streets the next day with headlines such as "STANLEY MATTHEWS BOMBSHELL," the reaction was extreme, not just in the Potteries but also, unsurprisingly, the news attracted the attention of other football clubs, several of which immediately expressed their interest in signing the young wizard. In Stoke, feelings ran so high that a protest meeting was called in the King's Hall. 3,000 people attended with another thousand unable to get in, and there was even talk of productivity being affected in the local factories. Under pressure, Matthews decided to stay and in a move to quash the rumours about resentment, the other players released a strongly-worded statement to the press:

> The players of Stoke City Football Club wish strongly to deny the unfounded rumours present in the district that there is trouble in the team. It has even been stated that there has been fighting among the players. These statements are absolutely ridiculous, and entirely baseless, and strongly resented by us.
> We wish to state publicly that complete harmony exists among ourselves. We do not wish to discuss the present position between the club and Stanley Matthews, but we think it only

fair to state that it has in no way affected our loyalty to the club and in particular to the manager, Mr. R. McGrory.

We strongly deny suggestions which have been made that we have any cause for complaint at the treatment we have received from the club and the management. At all times we have received fair and just treatment.

This is an entirely voluntary statement, issued by the senior team, with the approval of the whole playing and training staff.

The statement was signed by Arthur Turner, who was still the team captain, his deputy, Frank Soo, and several other members of the senior playing and coaching staff. Whether Frank's role was greater than this cannot be assumed, but he was made acting captain soon afterwards, in March 1938, and would become team captain in his own right during the following season when Turner, increasingly under pressure for his place from the younger Billy Mould, gave the armband up. There is no doubt that leadership was among Frank Soo's many positive qualities as a football player.

Despite the very poor start for Stoke, Frank appears to have had a good season himself in 1937/38, scoring four goals. The 1937 edition of the *Book of Football Stars* opined that "Soo is certain of international honours in the near future," and a letter to the *Evening Sentinel* from a Stoke City supporter, T. H. Wilson of Newcastle-under-Lyme expressed what was becoming a common view, and not only in Stoke-supporting circles: "Sir – As one who wrote asking that Stoke should spend money on new players, may I say, now that they have done so, how much I enjoyed their display at Wolverhampton. The home spectators were full of admiration about Stoke's cleverness and pretty football. May I also say that I have written to the '*Daily ___*' asking the Sports Editor to push the claims of Frank Soo for a place in the English international team. I have hopes that justice will be done for Soo. His last two games have been superb, and at Wolverhampton, it made you proud to have such a player in Stoke's side. All the home spectators were talking about him."

A little later, on 29 April 1938, a sports report in the same newspaper also brought up the subject of Frank Soo's claims for an international cap:

SOO SUPERB: CHANCE TO GO TO GERMANY?

Soo stood out so high above the others on Saturday that one wonders what he really has to do to be officially acknowledged the best wing-half in England today – he is already unofficially acknowledged to be that, on those grounds that have seen him in the last two or three months.

His right to international honours has been overlooked in the past in such a way that we are tired of hoping for the best for him.

Yet it must be permitted to mention that England want a team to play Germany on the Continent as soon as the season ends. And they will want to make changes from the one that made such a sorry show against Scotland.

Soo is playing better now, since taking Stoke's captaincy, than ever he has done in his career.

An old Stoke supporter tells me that in his opinion, with the possible exception of Jimmy Bradley [who] might be put on a par with him, Frank Soo [is] just now the best wing-half Stoke have EVER had.

Stanley Matthews should be a certainty for Germany. Are we to be once again disappointed, if we have a slender hope that Soo might be with him?

Simon Lowe, the Stoke City historian, suggests that Soo was unlucky not to be picked for England at this time: "The selectors persisted with less mercurial talents. It may even have been the case that Soo's international career was hampered by that of his team-mate Stanley Matthews. Picking more than one ball-artist undermined the 'progressive football,' based on a strong work ethic that the selectors sought to nurture."

Bob McGrory appointed Frank as permanent team captain for 1938/39. Stoke made a remarkable recovery in the second half of the season due in part, no doubt, because McGrory brought in some fresh faces, as well as transferring out some established players, like Scrimshaw to Middlesbrough (for £3,000) and Turner to Birmingham. Among the players that were brought in was a young Scot, Jock Kirton, from Banks O' Dee, of whom the *Aberdeen Journal* wrote in August 1937: "Even in these days of huge transfer fees an offer exceeding £5,000 for a reserve player is rather remarkable, Kirton has several times played in Stoke's league side, but he cannot maintain a regular place owing to the brilliance of Frank Soo." A very different type of player, Kirton would replace Soo at inside-left when Frank took Artur Tutin's place, and would go on to have a long and successful career for Stoke lasting until 1952.

In early October 1938, Stoke turned down an offer of £5,000 for Soo from their rivals Brentford. Rumours of Brentford's interest in him persisted for some time, but they came to nothing. On 9 October, Stoke were rewarded with a rare goal from their captain in their 3-1 win over Preston North End when he converted a short Matthews' free kick, smashing it off the underside of the bar from twenty-five yards out. The goal contributed to Stoke's first home victory that season. After that, things improved and they remained unbeaten from 29 October 1938 to the end of the season and finished in seventh place. It was around this time that a photograph was taken of Frank, watching a small boy kicking a football about. The lad was also being watched by fellow Stoke City stars, Joe Johnson, Freddie

Steele and Stanley Matthews, an impressive team of coaches for one so young. Although the *Encyclopaedia of Stoke City*, in which the photograph appears, identifies the boy as Frank's son, it was in fact his youngest brother, Kenneth, who was seventeen years younger than Frank and who would grow up to be a talented sportsman in his own right, playing Lancashire league cricket and briefly being on the books of Derby County, before having a career in the lower leagues at Ilkeston and elsewhere. Another brother, Ronnie, also appeared to have a football career ahead of him. Following in Frank's footsteps, he played for Liverpool schoolboys and Prescot Cables ("He is an inside-left and clubs are angling for him," claimed one newspaper) and was also tipped for footballing honours.

As part of one of the best teams at the highest level in the English football league, popular and at the peak of his powers, the clamour for Frank Soo to be awarded an international cap was becoming too loud to be ignored for very much longer. The *Daily Express*, among others, pressed his claims, to little apparent effect: "And what price Frank Soo?" Asked the *Express'* sports correspondent. "I put his name forward with great reserve because I fear there is little chance of the selectors picking him, despite the fact that he is an English-born player. I have said for three years that Soo, of Stoke, is one of the finest halves in the game, and it would be no less than he was worth if they put him in."

In January 1939, McGrory had planned that the Stoke City team should have some relaxation time at the spa in Buxton, close to Fairfield where Frank was born, but the trip had to be cancelled at the last minute because of drifting snow. The team was full of injured players including Matthews. Frank's efforts on a mud-bath of a pitch in a Third Round FA Cup match against Leicester City again won him national attention. The *Daily Herald* thought that "Stoke's star, in fact, was Soo, who timed his passes far better than any other player, and his ability to keep his feet when others slid and stumbled was something to marvel at," and the *Staffordshire Sentinel* believed that Soo's performance would long be remembered. His goal, which was something of a fluke, after it fell and stuck in the mud at his feet, and he thumped it past the Leicester goalkeeper from twenty yards, knocked the stuffing out of their opponents and earned Stoke a replay (which they lost). Having been moved to right half-back to replace the injured Massey, no one could accuse Soo of not being either accommodating or versatile at this time. He seems to have been able to play an effective and attractive style of football all over the field. Whether the constant changes affected his international chances is uncertain, but it may well have been a negative factor. Soo himself may have thought it did, as he became increasingly frustrated at being asked to play out of position.

In March 1938, Freda was ill and the local newspaper suggested that this was an explanation of his recent loss of form, ignoring the fact that he was playing on the right wing, filling in for yet another injured player: "In fairness to Frank Soo, Stoke's popular captain, who has recently been affected by a loss of form, it should be stated that his domestic circumstances have had a marked bearing on this position. Mrs Soo, unfortunately, has been seriously ill for some weeks, and she recently underwent an operation. Everyone will extend sympathy to the player and his wife, together with best wishes for Mrs Soo's complete recovery." The newspaper was able to report Freda's "complete recovery" and discharge from hospital a week later.

At the end of March, the club's chairman, Alderman Harry Booth, who had replaced A. J. C. Sherwin in fairly acrimonious circumstances in 1936, presented benefit cheques, for £650, to Frank and three other long-standing Stoke City players Fred Steele, Arthur Tutin and Bob Liddle at a meeting of the Directors at the Victoria Ground. A further £500 was awarded to Arthur Turner, who had recently transferred to Birmingham City. The Chairman's remarks may have been made with the recent dispute with Stanley Matthews in mind: "The payment of maximum benefits was only possible through Stoke being in the top-flight of football, said Mr Booth, and every effort must be made to keep the club in that position. Despite the talk about increased wages for footballers, wages and benefits had to be paid largely out of 'gate' revenue, and revenue depended on the class and standard of football provided for the spectators. The Stoke Directors desired always to recognise efficient and loyal service. Mr Booth referred to the happy relations existing throughout the club, and said the four players concerned in the presentations were a credit to Stoke and an example to the younger players."

As club captain, Frank replied on behalf of the players, telling the directors that they "would continue to give their best standard of service, and they appreciated the family spirit existing throughout the club. He himself, had been extremely happy at Stoke, and the players appreciated the interest of the directors and officials in their welfare."

Frank's fame was beginning to spread far and wide, including to Hong Kong, where a newspaper reported on 5 October 1938 that "Frank Soo, Buxton-born footballer of Chinese extraction, is this year's captain of Stoke City's first League side. Nicknamed 'Smiler,' Soo has been playing for the first team since he was 18 and such has been his form this season that more than one critic has pointed out, for the benefit of the England selectors, that Soo has all the playing qualifications necessary to represent England in international matches." It can safely be said that during this stage of Frank Soo's professional career, the clamour for his selection as an England international was worldwide.

By April 1939, it was becoming increasingly obvious that Stoke's proposed summer tour of Germany was not going to happen and attempts were made to organize a return match against Racing Club de Paris, who had come to England the previous year. Meanwhile, despite the increasing gravity of the political situation in Europe, life in the Potteries continued much as usual. In the same month, Soo and Fred Steele were linesman for the annual match between Stoke City and a Longton League XI played on the St Michael's ground at Stone. Stanley Matthews was the referee. Proceeds of the match were to go to the Longton Hospital. Frank, as team captain, also presented trophies at a charity schoolboys' match at Goldenhill, which had been kicked off by Matthews. In May 1939, despite being part of a losing side in another fundraising game, the Chesterfield Hospital Cup, Soo was described as "outstanding" and the "brainy player of the side" by the local press. Even Frank's life off the football field continued to fascinate the British public. A national publication, *Guide and Ideas*, published an interview with him about his "romance" with Freda:

AUTOGRAPH ROMANCE

> She was an ardent football fan and sent an autograph album for all the team to sign. In that way she met Frank Soo, of Stoke City – a meeting that was to lead to their marriage.
>
> Frank Soo, who threw up work in a laundry to become a footballer, tells the story of his romance in this week's *Guide and Ideas*.

Frank Soo had achieved a kind of stardom that was still rare in football at that time. He had become a genuine working-class hero, admired for his brilliance on the football field and his character off it. The references to his Chinese heritage were still being made, but less and less frequently. The summer of 1939 seems to have been filled with simple pleasures, as the *Sentinel* described: "With limited official duties, golf is claiming a good deal of the time of Stoke's players. This week interesting matches have been played between Mr McGrory, Soo, Steele, Sale, Peppitt, Ormston, Westland and Turner, the club's former centre-half. ... To his golfing activities, Frank Soo, Stoke's captain, has added bowls, and I hear that he has become a member of Oakhill Bowling Club."

Events in Europe were becoming increasingly ominous, however, and Stoke City's planned pre-season tour to Poland and Germany was finally cancelled. Better news was that on 24 August 1939, Stoke City announced that Frank Soo, now officially described as a right half-back, had been reappointed club captain for the 1939/40 season. The date has another, more far-reaching significance, however, as it was on this day that the Molotov-Ribbentrop non-aggression pact between Nazi Germany and the USSR was signed, making war in Europe almost inevitable as Germany saw its chance to expand its power further into Eastern Europe without the fear of having to face the Soviet army. The following day the British Prime

Minister, Neville Chamberlain, told the House of Commons that Britain was "in imminent peril of war." Nevertheless the Football League decided that football would continue normally, announcing: "Unless the crisis takes a turn for the worse we are carrying on as usual, so Saturday's matches will take place."

The government had different ideas, however. When war was declared the Football League realized that, with the likelihood of petrol rationing and the mass mobilization of the male population, the 1939/40 fixture list was no longer tenable and it was suspended. The three matches Stoke had already played in the 1939/40 season, against Charlton Athletic, Bolton Wanderers and Middlesbrough would be redesignated as "abandoned." Players took on war work until they could join up and serve their country in the armed forces. They remained eager to play for their own clubs, or for any clubs, and when the government eventually realized that football could be morale-boosting for soldiers and civilians alike, fixtures were arranged to fit in with the players' military commitments. Despite the guarantee to players that they would be able to return to their home clubs when the war was over, by the time that hostilities ceased, and players were released from the armed forces, six or seven years had elapsed. Many footballers' careers would be at an end by the time they returned to their own clubs. Some would receive life-changing injuries, all would be at least six years older. Life for everyone, including Frank Soo, would never be the same again.

3

'THE BEST RIGHT-HALF IN THE COUNTRY'
Britain and Europe, 1939 – 1945

Stoke City could hardly have chosen a worse destination for their planned tour of Europe in the summer of 1939 when they decided to visit Poland and Germany. The cancellation of this trip was the least concern for club, players and supporters alike. For some time before the official declaration of war was made by the Prime Minister, Neville Chamberlain, on 3 September 1939, the people of Britain had been aware that another conflict of global proportions was almost inevitable. Preparations had already been made for children to be evacuated from cities and gas masks were issued to the civilian population. It was assumed that most popular entertainments, including association football, would be suspended, probably for the duration of the war. The football authorities were determined that, unlike in 1914 which was still fresh in many people's memories, their sport would play - and be seen to be playing - its part in this conflict. Early in the First World War, professional footballers had come under a great deal of criticism for failing to join up and fight for their country when others were dying in their thousands. Many clubs had insisted that their contracts with players were honoured and the press attacked the young, fit men who chose to play football rather than do their patriotic duty. The attitude of most football clubs in 1939 was very different. Several took the decision to suspend their fixtures immediately. However, the government recognized very quickly that the most popular spectator sport in Britain, which tens of thousands of people flocked to watch every week, was an extremely valuable tool for keeping up the morale of a fearful civilian population and despite concerns that football grounds might even be targets for German bombers, it was a very short time before league football was allowed to return. Only Aston Villa, Derby County, Exeter City, Gateshead, Ipswich Town and Southampton decided to stop playing league football for the duration of the war. Many staff at other clubs, including players, were laid off as confusion arose about how the football league could continue in its pre-war form. Star players like Everton's Tommy Lawton were photographed signing on the dole.

On 21 August 1939, a few days before war was declared, the FA waived Rule 33, which stated that 'no player serving in His Majesty's Forces can be registered as a professional footballer.' As many footballers were intent on serving their country, this enabled a compromise to be made. Players could join the forces and still play for their clubs. Unfortunately it also had a negative effect on football because so many players wanted to do their bit in the war. They joined the armed forces in their hundreds and consequently many key players were unavailable to play for their clubs even before the war had begun. Squads were severely depleted because many players had joined up with Territorial Army units in preparation for the conflict to come. On 10 August the local newspaper in Stoke-on-Trent, the *Sentinel*, complained that McGrory did not even have enough players for a practice match, although despite his losses, he was still able to come up with some impressive names for City's next game. Soo, Matthews and Sale on one side played a team that featured Tutin, Franklin and Liddle. Frank Mountford, an inexperienced youngster, was brought in to play in the opposing side to Soo in that match and scored a goal. He was to become Soo's nemesis at the Victoria Ground, and over the course of the war, he would gradually displace Frank, preferred by McGrory despite - or perhaps because of - Soo's rising reputation as a player of international calibre.

The Stoke City players felt the effects of wartime conditions right from the start. On 2 September, the night before war was declared, the team had to travel back from Middlesbrough. Their game with Boro' had ended in a draw, two goals had been scored for each side, both of Stoke's by Tommy Sale. City had been able to field a strong side that also included Soo, Matthews, Tutin and Tennant. A blackout was in force for the long journey home by road and vehicles were only allowed to use side lights. The coach had to make its way through a tremendous storm. Following a terrifying six-hour crawl through the Pennines, the Stoke bus finally reached its destination at four o'clock on the morning that war was declared. After that, this fixture would not count for anything because it was one of the three League matches Stoke City had already taken part in that were cancelled by the Football League.

It took only six days from the declaration of war for football to make a comeback in the form of friendly matches, and the Football Association quickly received permission from the government to reinstate the game in some way. The Stoke City chairman, Alderman Harry Booth, was right behind the idea: "We feel that it would be a good thing for the public generally if football in some form or another be resumed. Stoke are ready at once to support any arrangements made by the FA and Football League." Regulations were drafted to ensure that football did nothing to impede the war effort, including a fifty-mile travel limit for teams (petrol saving was a particular obsession during the early years of the war), maximum crowd numbers of 15,000 and a ruling that no match could take place without the prior permission of the local police force. Later, as fears of direct attacks on football crowds by the Luftwaffe diminished, the restrictions were relaxed to allow twice as many spectators and some grounds were even used as air raid shelters. The Boothen End of the Victoria Ground - Stoke's Kop - became one huge shelter accommodating up to 400 people. The Butler Street Stand was used to store military equipment. Crowds, and therefore gate receipts, were substantially reduced anyway, because many fans - and players - were working in factories that no longer closed on Saturday afternoons and, as the war progressed, more and more supporters joined the armed forces and were posted far away from their home clubs.

Stoke embarked upon a series of friendlies, the first being a game between two local military units on 9 September, which one side - featuring Stoke players Peppitt, Mould and Massey, won 16-1. On 16 September Stoke played a friendly against Coventry City at the Victoria Ground, winning 3-1 and they beat local club Port Vale 3-2 on 23 September. McGrory had to negotiate with the Army every time to have players released. For the Coventry friendly, he managed to obtain permission for nineteen players (out of the sixty-four on Stoke's books) to be available. Despite losing Kirton, Jim and Doug Westland, Antonio, Wilkinson, Mould, Peppitt, Baker, Ormston, Massey and Brawley to the military, and Steele and Challinor to injuries (ostensibly incurred during Territorial Army training, but actually the result of fighting in boxing matches), Bob McGrory managed to scrape together a team from his remaining senior players and some of the local youngsters on Stoke's books. Frank Soo, aged 25, was firmly left in the position of leader and senior player, on and off the pitch, and Stoke were fortunate enough to be able to hang on to Stanley Matthews, at least for a while. The teams were now playing in numbered shirts - an innovation received with considerable supporter disgruntlement at the time. Whatever the rationale behind the change, it was to prove a useful tool for the next few years when supporters must have struggled to recognize half the players in their own ever-changing teams.

By 2 October 1939, the Football League had decided upon how league football should proceed during the war and it came up with plans for a War League. There were to be eight regional leagues to accommodate all but six of the eighty-eight pre-war league clubs. On 27 September the *Edinburgh Evening News* explained more about how the reorganization of the football leagues would look: "The Football League is now going ahead with the plans for grouping clubs into regional sections, but it is not expected that competitive football will be resumed before October 14. It is understood there will be seven groups, and none will include more than 18 clubs. Sections are likely to be: London (16), Manchester (12), Midlands (12), North-western (12), North-eastern (10), South and West Yorkshire (10), and West (10)." Stoke City were put into the Western Regional League along with Chester, Crewe Alexandra, Everton, Liverpool, Manchester City, Manchester United, New Brighton, Port Vale, Stockport County, Tranmere Rovers, and Wrexham. Stoke had not played Wrexham since 1927 and New Brighton for even longer. The players' fees were set by the club at £2 per match. However, the Football Association ordered that the amount should be reduced to thirty shillings. This set off a dispute about wages between the Players' Union and the Football League that went on throughout the war. There is little doubt, given the determination he showed throughout his career to stand up for players' rights, that Frank Soo would have been one of the players who was most vocal on this subject.

The onset of war began to have an immediate effect on everyone's lives, although oddly, Stoke-on-Trent was not considered to be an industrial target either by the British authorities or the Luftwaffe. Players and spectators alike were either expected to join the services or enrol for essential war work, such as coal mining and engineering. Employers were not inclined to allow anyone time off for football, not even the famous Stanley Matthews. Professional footballers were often quite desperate to do something for their country while waiting for their call-up papers to come through. On 15 September 1939, the *Evening Sentinel* reported that: "Most footballers without waiting for any decision on the future of football, set out to find themselves new jobs. Stanley Matthews has secured a position, but will be free for football. Tom Sale, Clem Smith and Arthur Tutin have taken jobs with the Corporation Public Works Dept., which is responsible for civil defence work – making shelters, digging trenches, et cetera." Stan Matthews probably spoke for most footballers when he described the problems he had finding wartime employment: "I tried for many jobs but when I was asked what experience I had, my chances were nil. I went straight into football from school and had never learned any trade." Matthews eventually found work in a local brass foundry.

By 27 September, the FA agreed that players should be allowed to play for any other club in England and Wales provided their own clubs were agreeable. This would eventually lead to most of the leading players of the day swapping teams from time to time to appear as guest players. Frank would "guest" for a great many clubs between 1941 and 1945, including Everton and Chelsea. In the early days of the war, however, the proposal caused yet another disagreement between the Stoke City board and Stanley Matthews, which as usual dominated the newspaper headlines. Matthews - ever conscious of his own financial interests and the power that he had over his employers because he could literally add thousands to a crowd if he was playing - applied for permission to play for Port Vale or Crewe Alexandra on the days when Stoke were away. He wasn't able to leave the foundry on time to travel any great distance to matches. This would mean Matthews would still be able to claim a match fee from Crewe or Vale by turning out for them. Stoke City's directors considered it to be an outrageous suggestion and quickly refused to give Matthews permission on the grounds that they did not want their star player benefiting any other clubs, as both Vale and Crewe had become unlikely rivals in the new Western league. Stoke decided to instead ask Matthews' employers to release him early so that he could play in away matches, but they were understandably not prepared to do so and England's star footballer had to spend many Saturday afternoons on the sidelines. He was missed. As well as having an effect on crowd numbers, his absence probably contributed to the disastrous 6-0 defeat in a friendly match against West Bromwich Albion at the Hawthorns on 30 September. Stoke had to make do with Syd Peppitt filling in for Matthews. Despite Soo narrowly missing a goal with a fine header, City were overwhelmed by a WBA side which contained an old teammate, Joe Johnson. Wartime friendly or not, it seemed that pre-war rivalries were as fierce as they had ever been. It was also becoming increasingly obvious how severely wartime conditions were going to affect football for supporters and players alike. As well as blackouts and travel restrictions, the Chief Constable of Staffordshire wrote to West Bromwich Albion, with some stringent instructions: "All vehicles must be parked in private car parks in order to keep the roads clear for essential services. Spectators must distribute themselves evenly on the stands and on the terraces, and are requested not to pack behind the goals. If an air raid warning is received they must take cover in the stands in an orderly manner, keep calm and do all they can to avoid panic. The continuance of football depends upon the strict observance of these conditions."

Despite losing thirteen professionals early on, McGrory was relatively lucky in that several of his star players at first got jobs in local factories, but if players thought this would make it easier for them to continue as usual, they were mistaken. Their war work commitments meant long hours and little flexibility was offered to them so that they could take time off to travel to matches. Ever watchful of the whereabouts of Stoke's popular captain, the local newspaper, the *Evening Sentinel,* reported on 7 October 1939: "Soo should be available [for the next game] as it is hoped he has now secured a permanent job at the same works as Brigham." This was at the British headquarters of the Michelin tyre company in Campbell Road, Stoke-on-Trent where Frank worked in the engineering department alongside teammates Harry Brigham and Tommy Sale until he finally joined the armed forces.

Frank played in the next two friendlies, the first against Manchester United at the Victoria Ground on 7 October 1939, a 2-2 draw, the second also at home, against Birmingham, which Stoke won 3-2. A sign of the times was that he was moved to the right half-back position for both games, replacing an injured Alf Massey. This became normal for Soo during the rest of his time playing for the club. He appears to have been extremely flexible and loyal when it came to turning out for fixtures at all levels. Throughout the war he demonstrated his willingness to play in four different positions (left full-back, right half-back, left half-back and inside-left) to accommodate the problems caused by gaps in McGrory's depleted squad. By doing so, he may have done his chances of being picked for England a great deal of harm - an obvious criterion for international selection is that a footballer has made a particular role or position his "own" - and it also meant that younger players were able to displace him particularly towards the end of the war when he was older and increasingly unavailable to Stoke City because of other commitments. His loyalty was publicly appreciated, but not rewarded, by Bob McGrory and it is clear that by the end of the war Frank keenly felt that he had been badly treated by his manager and the Stoke City board.

By Saturday, 21 October 1939, competitive football had resumed, albeit in a very different form. The *Sheffield Telegraph* expressed the kind of ambiguous feelings about the return of league football that were probably common enough among everyone involved in the sport. Under the headline "SCATTERED STARS LEVEL TEAMS," it cautiously welcomed football back: "Competitive football is to be resumed today on as ambitious a scale as wartime conditions permit and though no one expects the standards of normal times, or intense excitement, the entertainment will be satisfying." Stoke's first match in the War League was against Everton at Goodison Park, a game that ended as a 4-4 draw. City had been 4-1 down at half-time but were rescued by a second half hat-trick by Tommy Sale who was in the form of his life that season, scoring 37 goals. Frank was back on the left wing and the *Evening Sentinel* reported "In the absence of Matthews' wizardry, the ball-play of Soo, Ormston and Liddle and the tricks of Tutin gave the crowd so much appreciated entertainment." The match was typical of wartime league football in that it featured a lot of goals and was not a true reflection of the state of those clubs in peacetime. It was a bizarre league in which Stoke might play Manchester United or Everton one week and New Brighton or Port Vale the next. As the war went on, the absence of star players through military service and the phenomenon of guest footballers meant that some big clubs conceded spectacular defeats and lesser clubs had surprising successes. One match, on Christmas Day 1940, between Norwich City and Brighton and Hove Albion would end with a scoreline of 18-0. The scorer of six of Norwich's goals, Ipswich Town's Fred Chadwick would spend much of the rest of war in a Japanese prisoner of war camp.

Frank scored a rare goal in the 54th minute of Stoke's second league match against Stockport County (whom they had not played since the 1926/27 season) on 28 October. City won 4-2 in front of a much reduced home crowd of 2,000. In a match dominated by Stoke's rampant attacking play Soo's goal, which quickly followed one by Matthews, was a well-placed header from a free kick which defeated the County goalkeeper. Although it was looking as if Stoke City were going to have a good season, McGrory was aware that too many of his key players were not going to be able to play regularly and he took action. Eight days after the 4-1 defeat of New Brighton on 11 November 1939, Stoke signed Neil Franklin, Frank Bowyer, Jock McCue, Ted Wordley and Frank Mountford. McGrory's plan to survive the war, he said, was to try to sign players "from a seven-mile radius" of Stoke-on-Trent. He struck lucky in finding Franklin, who was from Shelton in the Potteries. He would go on to become one of Stoke City's finest players and another England international. In his autobiography, *Soccer at Home and Abroad*, Franklin would remember Frank Soo as "one of the grandest wing-halves and greatest fellows you could wish to meet." When selecting his favourite players, Franklin chose him as one of his all-time XI - he picked Matt Busby as right half and Soo on the left and wrote: "For the other wing-half I would pick Frank Soo. Frank was always a better player than he was given credit for, and in my early days he helped me a lot. He would be the perfect partner for Matt Busby, despite the intense competition he gets from such people as Joe Mercer."

Despite the upheaval of war, life was continuing as usual in many ways and on 2 December 1939, the *Sentinel* announced that Frank had attended the "annual prize distribution and smoking concert" of the Oakhill Bowls and Recreation Club in Stoke-on-Trent. He was awarded second prize in the main tournament, losing out to one W. Brunt who took the first prize. Frank's immense competitive streak ensured that he took every sport and pastime very seriously. On 9 December Frank was again playing for Stoke City, this time against a club from his home town. It was a tough match in torrential rain in front of a paltry 500 spectators and Stoke didn't even know who would be playing in their first team until a few minutes before kick-off. Nevertheless they managed to beat Liverpool by three goals to one. Soo should have scored early on, but his brilliant shot from an Ormston corner was saved when the Reds' defender Tennant headed the ball out from under the bar. The match report in the *Liverpool Evening Express* described Soo as "seeking all opportunities for shots," but he was unlucky and failed to find the net.

Over the Christmas period, Stoke played another series of friendly matches, first playing Sheffield Wednesday on 16 December at Hillsborough. The continuing saga of whether or not Stanley Matthews would turn out for Stoke once again dominated the headlines. Clubs were often desperate for Matthews to play because his presence massively increased their gate receipts. On this occasion he did play, and Stoke City won 2-1, but the doubt about his appearance lasted right up until the match and meant a lower crowd than hoped for turned up. "It was painful to see the many blank spaces on all sides," reported the *Sheffield Evening Telegraph*. Soo, who was picked out by the Sheffield press as "a fine player," had to play out of position to accommodate changes made after Griffiths moved to outside-left having been slightly injured early on in the match. He did not have a great game, struggling with Wednesday's winger, Massarella. He was now being described as a utility player, which was a rather unkind reward for his willingness to fill in the gaps in the team. A second friendly had been arranged against Lincoln City at Sincil Bank on 23 December 1939, which the *Lincolnshire Echo* greeted with some excitement: "Lincoln City have been fortunate in securing Stoke City as visitors to Sincil Bank tomorrow in the first of the Christmas games. Even in a friendly game, Stoke are an undoubted attraction, and this should be the pick of the holiday fixtures, for the Potters are sending a side of First Division standard. Unfortunately Stanley Matthews, the Stoke wizard of the right wing, will not after all be able to come to Lincoln. ... There are other players in the Stoke side. The visitors will have the services of Soo, a brilliantly adaptable footballer, born of Chinese parents in England..."

After a long trip to Lincoln, the Stoke City players arrived just before kick-off only to find that the referee had called the match off. Heavy snowfall not only meant that it was impossible to play but the team had a difficult journey back to the Potteries. Held up by drifting snow, it took them more than seven hours to get home. Even so, the club had a long dispute with Lincoln City over their £35 match fee and ended up only receiving £7 expenses. Such soul-destroying trips for friendlies must have taken their toll and Stoke lost their home and away matches against Bolton Wanderers on Christmas Day and Boxing Day, both of which Frank played in, 3-0 (away) and 5-1 (home) respectively. In a friendly at Bury on 30 December, they lost 7-6, despite drawing 1-1 at half-time and another hat-trick from Tommy Sale. It must have been a remarkable match to watch, and to play in, as in two separate spells of six and then eight minutes, ten goals were scored. Bury were a strong side, undefeated in their previous eleven games, but the score didn't prevent the *Sentinel* correspondent "Potter" from opining that a draw would have been the right result. It was an exhausting Christmas period for Soo, who played in all these games and presumably also carried on working at Michelin. By Christmas 1939, Stoke City had managed to retrieve eleven points from eight games - despite losing most of their best players to the war effort - and they were in fourth place in the Western regional league, only a point behind Manchester City, Everton and Manchester United.

Frank missed the first game of the New Year, a league match against Tranmere. He wasn't injured so it's possible McGrory allowed him a well-earned break and some precious time with his wife. Freda kept her hairdressing salon, in Glebe Street, Stoke-on-Trent, open throughout the war and, perhaps unusually for the time, she ran it under the name she used before her marriage, Miss F. Lunt. She appears to have been an independent woman, with a strong network of family and friends in North Staffordshire, but Frank's frequent absences, which became more and more common as the war ground on, would have put a strain on many newly married couples. Freda was luckier than many wives, however, and never had to worry about her man being posted abroad, or being taken as a prisoner of war or hearing that he was missing in action.

On 19 January 1940, the *Daily Mirror* visited the Victoria Ground and reported on the state of affairs at the Potteries club:

THEY GO WITHOUT TEA TO TRAIN

When boy-footballers of 16 and 17, after a hard days' work in an armament factory, forego their tea and travel several miles to do sprints and gymnasium work in the black-out, you can take it they are keen on keeping fit. The boys who do this, two nights a week, are the young professionals and juniors on Stoke City's staff. The older professionals do it, too, and this voluntary training has delighted Mr R. McGrory, the Stoke manager. Frank Soo, the Stoke captain, cycles seven miles to his home after the work-outs. Ace winger Stan Matthews, too, is always one of the party, for he pays strict attention to keeping himself fit.

Stoke's home form continued to be strong in the second half of the season, but the squad was usually weakened for away matches and with the frequent absence of Matthews, they did not perform as well. McGrory was determined to continue using his youngsters rather than relying on finding suitable guest players: "I intend playing the regular members of the club for as long as possible," he told the press. "It is the only fair thing for the available players. Moreover if and when first-team vacancies occur, Stoke have splendid reserves in Franklin, Mountford, Hampson and Bowyer. These young players are ready for a promotion at any time." Stoke's supporters, however, did not always appreciate the absence of their favourite stars, often booing their replacements, like poor Syd Peppitt who would usually take Stanley Matthew's place on the right wing when the Wizard was unavailable. As the war continued and the Luftwaffe began its bombing campaign in earnest, it became increasingly difficult for players serving in the forces to travel. This was not because of objections from their new military masters. As soon as he arrived at his RAF unit near Blackpool, Stanley Matthews' Commanding Officer informed him that it was now official War Office policy to allow footballers to carry on playing as it had been accepted that they could better help the war effort this way. Frank was to be stationed at the same camp later on and presumably encountered the same attitude. Many professional footballers spent the war as Physical Training Instructors (PTIs), although some saw enemy action and fourteen professional footballers lost their lives. Only one Stoke City player was killed during the Second World War, reserve team player Francis Carpenter.

Matthews' CO was true to his word and, in the early part of the war, Stan managed to play in almost all of Stoke's matches. City travelled to Anfield on 6 April 1940. The first goal was scored for Liverpool from twenty yards by Frank's old teammate from West Derby, Jack Balmer. Steele equalized by heading in a cross from Matthews and Stoke won the match after a piece of luck when Balmer hit the post, the rebound falling to Jock Kirton who, via Liddle, put Peppitt through on goal. The 2-1 victory put Stoke into a strong position in the Western Division championship with twenty-seven points, one ahead of Manchester United. On 18 May, Stoke travelled up to Goodison Park for a third round War League Cup match against another team that had been interested in the teenage Soo. Bob McGrory told the press: "This is going to be the best cup-tie of the round, and I am bringing along a team which I firmly believe can win. ... The City, as well as Everton, will have out practically a pre-war team." Stoke would have the services of six of their Army players – Wilkinson, Mould, Turton, Peppitt, Steele and Ormston, as well as Stan Matthews and Frank Soo. In the event Steele didn't play. Everton were planning to put out a team containing nine international players, including Joe Mercer and Tommy Lawton. McGrory added: "If the people do not come to see this match then there must be something wrong somewhere." Those Liverpudlians who did heed McGrory's advice were able to see Everton beat Stoke by a single penalty.

After three more games, in which Soo played but did not score, the Potters would eventually win the War League Western Division with thirty-one points, two points above Liverpool. In his first season of the war, Frank would play twenty-eight games (three in the old league, twenty in the War League and five in the replacement for the FA Cup, the War Cup) plus twelve friendlies. Never prolific, he scored only three times. As team captain, Frank would be a permanent presence in the Stoke City side during the 1940/41 season until he was taken off with a groin injury in the last game, a 3-2 defeat of Manchester United at the Victoria Ground. His fitness problems would not be fully resolved until he had surgery at the North Staffordshire Royal Infirmary in January the following year. Despite having won their league the previous season, things were no longer looking good for City. On 3 June 1940 McGrory told his board of directors that almost half of his fifty-four retained players, most of them professionals, were no longer available and a further ten would only be able to play on occasions. The manager would have to use all his undoubted canniness for Stoke City to remain competitive during the rest of the war. The 1941/42 season began therefore with Stoke's player resources being stretched to the limit, but the Football League had decided to change the structure of the divisions yet again. Stoke would now be playing in League North. Soo would only make nine league appearances during this season, plus three in the qualifying rounds of the League Cup. He had come back from his surgery, helping to rehabilitate himself by turning out as a guest player for Newcastle United and McGrory publicly praised Soo, who continued to make the effort to play for City whenever he could. In contrast, Matthews was falling out of favour with his manager who was frustrated that his star did not appear to be trying very hard to get to Stoke's games. McGrory even noted in his records that Soo, who was then at the same RAF base as Matthews (RAF Kirkham, near Blackpool) had "at least made the effort to travel to Stoke to play for his own club whenever he could." According to Stoke City historian, Simon Lowe, "Matthews made no such effort." Despite, his loyalty, Frank would himself experience a similar souring of his relationship with McGrory after the war was over.

Frank was among the last of the 1938/39 Stoke City team to be called up when he joined the Royal Air Force on 28 July 1941 and like Stanley Matthews, Leading Aircraftman Soo (service number 1539029) remained the idol of Stoke City supporters. In his account of Stoke's wartime years, *Potters at War*, Simon Lowe quotes a young fan, Owen Bennion, who recalled: "You never knew who was actually going to be playing. One day I turned up at the ground to see a young lad running towards us excitedly shouting 'Soo's here. Soo's here!' It was always so thrilling to see the likes of Soo, Matthews and Steele when they could make it back to play and if word got around it could add a lot to the gate at the last minute." Frank's dedication to Stoke City was impressive. One report of Soo playing against Crewe Alexandra - called away to play for Stoke from a guest appearance for Everton at short notice - described how he had to "catch the 3.15 am train on Sunday morning and cycle eighteen miles to get back to his unit in time for reveille at 0730 hours."

Frank Soo's RAF service record is not very informative about his wartime activities, although we do know that he did not become a PTI like many professional footballers, but served in the same way that most ordinary civilians did, apart from the fact that he continued to play football - a great deal of football. On 28 July 1941 he arrived at 3RC [3 Recruit Centre] which was at RAF Padgate, in a suburb of Warrington in Lancashire. Padgate was one of the national recruitment centres and thousands of new entrants to the RAF were processed there during the war, but it was also close to Liverpool where presumably Frank could visit Quan, Beatrice and the rest of his family. Like every other serviceman, Frank would have been given a medical and other tests to help the RAF decide where he would be best placed to serve. All his subsequent service appears to be connected with technical training, particularly in the training of aircrew in the skills of beam approach. The locations of the RAF stations at which he was based during the war such as RAF Feltwell, near Thetford in Norfolk, and RAF Croughton in Northamptonshire seem to confirm that this was his RAF trade. The Beam Approach Beacon System (BABS) was a state-of-the-art method of enabling aircraft to land blind at night, which itself used another relatively new invention, RADAR, to communicate between a vehicle on the runway and a transponder in the aircraft.

Next Frank was sent to a second Recruitment Centre at RAF Whitley Bay for a short time but by August 1941 he was at 10 S of TT (School of Technical Training) at RAF Kirkham. No 10 School of Technical Training had been formed in March 1940 with the intention of training flight mechanics and riggers. Once again, he was based not too far from his parents' home in Liverpool, but he was also close enough to get back to Stoke-on-Trent if required. He was handy for the Liverpool clubs too, of course, who were by then actively seeking guest players.

During the 1941/42 season, Frank began to combine playing for Stoke City with guest appearances for other clubs, as well as playing for various RAF XIs and Football Association representative teams. He certainly made an impact in his home town as he turned out as a guest for both Liverpool and Everton. On 15 October 1941, the *Liverpool Evening Express* reported that "Mr George Kay, Manager of Liverpool, is not letting a touch of influenza prevent him continuing his quest for star players. He is hopeful that three new guest players will be on duty at Anfield on Saturday against Stockport County. Included in the list of 13 players are Frank Soo, the Stoke City captain; Clarke, the Manchester City full-back now in the Royal Air Force and Whittaker, the Kingstonian amateur centre-half. ... Frank Soo, the Stoke City half-back and former Liverpool schoolboy player, is included among the seven forwards named, and the Kopites will have the first opportunity of seeing Ainsley, the Leeds United forward, assisting Liverpool. It is expected that Soo will play at outside-left as partner to Dorsett." In the event, Frank did not play for Liverpool who beat Stockport by six goals to one.

Frank was still travelling back home to the Potteries to play for Stoke as often as he was allowed to, turning out, for example, in the League North matches on 18 October 1941 versus Manchester City and on 25 October against Manchester United. He helped Stoke beat City 5-0 but they only managed a draw with United. On 15 November he was back at the Victoria Ground helping his club defeat New Brighton, the club that had rejected him ten years earlier following a trial match. The 4-0 win must have given him at least a little bit of satisfaction. All this football, and Frank was now also being called upon to play in representative teams by both the RAF and the Football Association. He was selected to play in an RAF XI to play the FA at Bristol on 22 November 1941. It would be the first of many representative matches that would take him all over Britain and, at the end of the war, to mainland Europe. That match was followed by another league game back up in the north west against Tranmere on 29 November. The local press greeted the possibility of watching the former Liverpool schoolboy star excitedly. Although Frank didn't get on the score sheet, he impressed the 2,000 strong crowd as the travelling Stoke side beat Tranmere by seven goals to two. A few days later Frank was selected for an RAF XI, to play at Leeds along with other luminaries of the game such as Arsenal's Eddie Hapgood and Blackpool's Jock Dodds. Sixty-four players had already been picked for the many RAF teams that were playing around the country, often raising funds for hospitals or the war effort, but Soo was still being picked out by the press as the famous name. Sometimes (although increasingly less often) it was because his Chinese ancestry was still thought to be an interesting point but generally he was singled out because he had become a favourite with reporters and fans all over the country. At this point in his career, he could accurately be described as a household name. What now looks like a remarkable photograph was taken around this time of a sextet of famous footballers, all dressed in RAF uniform, peering out of an aircraft door. They were Joe Mercer, Jack Taylor, Frank Swift, Stanley Matthews Matt Busby and Frank Soo. If anything indicates the place that Frank Soo held in popular esteem in the early 1940s, surely that photograph in the company of some of Britain's greatest players does.

On 6 December 1941 Stoke played Stockport County in League North and once again Frank was able to play as he was stationed in the area. He contributed two goals to Stoke's 6-1 victory. He was again selected, along with Preston's Bill Shankly, to represent the RAF, this time against an Army XI at Ayr on New Year's Day, 1942. The Scottish newspaper, the *Sunday Post*, reported:

> Jimmy M'Grory [the former Scotland manager] was rushing along to the dressing-room at the finish to congratulate 'young Paterson' [the Celtic player, George Paterson]. And, by the way, Jimmy took a great notion to Frank Soo, the RAF's Anglo-Chinese inside-left.
>
> 'I could be doing with him at Rugby Park for after the war,' said Jimmy. A M'Grory will get him all right. But it will be Bob M'Grory, of Stoke. Frank was the crowd number one favourite – and remember there were nineteen internationalists on the field.

His appearance that year in an RAF XI against the Metropolitan Police at Wembley Stadium was just one of many matches. Bryan Hawkins, who was a ball boy at Wembley often during this period, had a good reason to remember Frank Soo when he was interviewed years later for a book about the Wartime and Victory Internationals called *Forgotten Caps*:

> During the war, the ballboys for the matches played at Wembley Stadium were Boy Scouts picked from various Wembley troops,

and I was lucky enough to be selected four times including one match between the RAF and Police. At the Internationals, the ballboys waited in the tunnel, with the players, and then ran out just in front of the teams. We had strict instructions NOT to kick the ball back, but to always throw it or hand it to the players. During one match I attempted to retrieve the ball and throw it back to Frank Soo (Stoke City). Unfortunately, the ball struck part of the fence and bounced back onto the greyhound track. By this time Soo was snapping his fingers and shouting 'Hurry up, son!' I jumped over the fence, grabbed the ball, and threw it with great haste. This time it struck the linesman on the back of the head and rolled down the pitch. Soo decided to fetch it himself and Joe Mercer (England's captain) thought it was a great joke, as did most of the crowd. Was my face red!

I was a keen collector of sporting autographs and used to try and get the signatures on cigarette cards. Being a ballboy at Wembley, it gave me direct access to the players just before and after the match. I had a card of Joe Mercer, from the Wills' Association Footballers series, and he autographed it for me after the above match, but I didn't have the nerve to ask Frank Soo. So my Churchman's number 41 card, from the Association Footballers series, remained unsigned!

Bryan's perception of Soo's personality was probably unfortunate, although everyone who ever played with or for him will tell you how seriously he took his football. Frank's young neighbour back in Stoke-on-Trent, Alan Chadwick, however, remembers a very different man, who was immensely kind and would bring back mementos and autographs for him: "He gave me an England versus France programme signed by both teams and when he was playing for Stoke, he took my autograph book and got it signed by all the great players of the day. He continued to take it with him when he moved on to other clubs, including when he went to Scandinavia. Unfortunately I never got it back because I didn't see him again and he must have forgotten to send it to me."

By 3 January 1942, Frank was back in Stoke to play in what must have looked like a much more prosaic event than his RAF match in Scotland, a League Cup qualifying match against Walsall. The game appears to have been less mundane than expected however. Frank scored in the sixty-first minute, but his goal was overshadowed by Tommy Sale's ninth hat-trick of the season. In front of a big wartime crowd of 20,000, the game finished as an 8-0 rout of the Black Country minnows. Stoke were quickly brought back down to earth on 10 January in the next qualifying round of the League Cup, however, losing by four goals to nil at The Hawthorns. On 4 March 1942, AC Soo was sent to 11RC at Skegness for further training.

H. Jack Lazenby, who was there around the same time, painted a picture of what life there would have been like for Frank and many others in an interview he gave to the BBC website in 2005:

> Many of us were put in requisitioned houses. I was put into a house in Firbeck Avenue off the Drummond Road. I shared an upstairs room with an airframe fitter named Charlie Cork who came from Northampton. There were only two camp beds in the room. We were to be at Skegness for a month on what was called a Backers Up course. Butlins Holiday Camp had been taken over by the Government, and it was there we had our meals and on one or two occasions assembled in the camp theatre for a talk by an officer. At Skegness I met airmen I had known at Brize Norton and many that had been on the fitters' course at Blackpool.
>
> The Backers Up course consisted mostly of football, arms drill, firing on the rifle range, route marches and PT which most of us had done before. For arms drill we used rifles, but for other exercises that was playing at soldiers we used wooden rifles. Many of the beaches at Skegness were mined and surrounded with barbed wire and there were danger notices. As far as I can recollect we were free on Easter Sunday and Monday. There were few civilians or holiday makers about ...
>
> As most people know the air at Skegness is very bracing and at the end of the four weeks I felt pretty fit. Although it was war time there were plenty of fish and chips, beer and cigarettes although I was a non-smoker. I do not recall going to the cinema, but we went to a show at a theatre and saw and heard Rudi Starita and his girl band.

It's impossible to know whether Frank Soo caught that performance of Rudi Starita, but he would certainly have enjoyed the opportunity to do PT and play football.

If football was one of the main ways of passing the time at RAF Skegness, it would have been an enjoyable posting for Frank. He was close to Lincoln where on 13 March 1942 he was part of a strong RAF XI to play a friendly against Lincoln City at Sincil Bank. Once again it was Soo who was picked out by the local newspaper, the *Lincolnshire Echo*, as the main attraction: "Frank Soo is of Chinese extraction, and early attracted attention because of his brilliant play with Liverpool schoolboys. Stoke secured his services in the 1932-3 season in the face of strong competition, and he has proved a grand player either at forward or half-back."

Although he was still managing the occasional game for Stoke City, he was increasingly unavailable for his home club and on 11 April 1942 he guested for Millwall - and was made captain for the game - in the London Cup. Millwall defeated Aldershot 4-1, although losing their goalkeeper Briggs, during the match, who was taken to hospital with a suspected cracked fibula, couldn't have helped Millwall's opponents. It may have been Frank's appearances for the London side that drew the attention of the England selectors because it would not be long until he was finally picked to play, a selection which many supporters and commentators regarded as being extremely overdue. Nineteen days later, on 30 April, Frank had left the Lincolnshire coast for his next posting to 9AGS (Air Gunnery School) at RAF Llandwrog near Caernarfon (now the site of Caernarfon Airport). This station also appears to have been a centre for training in the flying and navigation of aircraft at night. It was certainly a more convenient location, as far as Frank was concerned, for travelling to play football. It was handier for playing for Stoke in League North, especially at places like Chester, but it was also much more convenient for Ninian Park, Cardiff, where Frank would finally play his first game as an England international.

Frank's first England call-up, when he represented his country against Wales at Cardiff on 9 May saw him playing in front of a crowd of 30,000, in a team that included Tommy Lawton and Arsenal's Edris Hapgood. Soo was in a rather experimental half-back line, with Cliff Britton of Everton and Coventry City's George Mason. William Lucas won the match for Wales with a goal in the twentieth minute. Soo was the only newcomer to the England team.

Having made a guest appearance for Liverpool earlier in the year, Frank was asked to play in an Everton side for a Lancashire Cup match in May 1942. According to George Orr's book, *Everton Football Club during World War Two*, Frank became a popular guest player for Liverpool's rivals: "Everton were out of the Cup ... Evertonians were not happy. Lancashire Senior Cup first leg 2nd Round gives Everton an away game at Manchester City. Everton try their best but with a weakened team they lose 2-0, 5000 watch. Seven days later and it's all to play for at Goodison in the 2nd leg. Everton have a surprise up their sleeve. New England International, Frank Soo, is a guest player for the Blues. He is signed to Stoke but makes his Everton debut today [on 16 May 1942]. ... He is a quality player. .... He made an excellent debut scoring two goals and helping Tommy Lawton get a hat trick in a 6-1 triumph. Anderson got the other goal for Everton. This was a truly unbelievable win as most Evertonians if they were honest would have said a draw would have been good. 18,000 fans had seen a new Everton star in Frank Soo but it would be hard to get him to play more often as he was a regular at Stoke City."

Although the Toffees fielded a team that included eight internationals that day, the *Liverpool Express* was most excited about the prospect of Frank Soo making his debut at Goodison:

Manchester City included Bacuzzi, the England and Fulham defender, against Everton in the second 'leg' of the Lancashire cup tie at Goodison Park today. Frank Soo, The Stoke City International, made his debut for Everton, appearing at inside-left with Stevenson on the wing.

Everton faced a two-goals deficit, the tie being decided on aggregate of the two games. ...

Everton opened on a top note, Stevenson and Soo combining neatly, but neither Lawton nor Bentham could quite get command of the centre. ... Soo broke through on his own and his low shot was turned around the post by Robinson. Soo created an opening for Bentham who, however, could not get the ball to his liking, and after some brilliant work by Bentham and Anderson had produced a corner, Keen burst through with an 18-yarder which swung outside. ... In 25 minutes Everton took the lead through Lawton, to reduce the deficit to a goal. This was a spectacular goal, Soo nodding the ball across for Lawton to sweep by Walker and drive high into the net. ... Soo brought art and effectiveness to the Everton attack, and he went through on his own only for Robinson to come out and smother the shot. So far as forward play was concerned this was Everton's best for many weeks.

The half-time score was Everton 2, Manchester City 0.
The newspaper report continued:

Everton resumed strongly, and when Soo and Stevenson got the City defence in a state of bewilderment, Soo pushed the ball over for Bentham to try and stab it home, but Robinson saved magnificently. ...

Two more corners came as a reward of progressive building up, and then, in 61 minutes, Soo placed Everton further ahead and on terms in the aggregate. Stevenson drew the defence for Soo to run on and lob the ball into the net over Robinson's head as the goalkeeper advanced. ... Robinson was playing brilliantly in the city goal, saving from Bentham and Lawton, before Bacuzzi turned the ball off Soo's foot as he was about to shoot. Everton continued to hammer at the city goal, but Walker and his colleagues were brilliant in their resistance. It was not until the 81st minute that Everton made the score 4-1, and so took the lead in the tie.

Soo not only started the movement but was there to finish it. Taking over from Keen he sent Stevenson through and

Stevenson, instead of centring, slipped the ball inside for Soo to place low into the net.

Two days later, the local press revived the complaint, now almost traditional, that Merseyside clubs had made a terrible mistake in letting this local talent go:

SOO'S HAPPY DEBUT

Apart from a short period just after the interval Everton rarely looked in danger of defeat at the hands of Manchester City on Saturday. By that time Tom Lawton and Alf Anderson had wiped out the City's two-goal start, but then Boothway restored a City advantage with a goal savouring strongly of offside, but which came through Everton slackness.

It was Frankie Soo, the Stoke City international, operating at inside-left with Stevenson on the wing, who finally broke down that City resistance crowning a neat Keen-Stevenson-Soo move with a winning shot, and it was Soo who scored again just after to place Everton definitely on the victory road and so make his debut for Everton a memorable one. ...

Yes, altogether a nice contribution from a revived Everton – and please, Mr Kelly, let's have more of Frank Soo, a boy who should never have been allowed to leave Merseyside to gain football fame.

Frank played for Everton again on 30 May and 12 September. This second match, a Liverpool derby, which both Mercer and Lawton had to miss because they were with the Army FA touring side, was remarkable in that as well as having Frank Soo as a guest, it introduced another half-Chinese player, seventeen-year-old, Jason Scott-Lee from Rhyl in north Wales. A graduate of Liverpool University, Scott-Lee (whose granddaughter Lisa would find fame as a member of the pop group Steps in the late 1990s) was an extremely talented footballer who had been on the books of Manchester United. He impressed in this match, giving a local newspaper another opportunity to point out that Merseyside should never have lost Frank Soo: "I do not think that two Chinese players have ever played for one club on the same day," wrote their football correspondent, presumably only considering British football. "Curiously enough, both will be at inside-left. Scott-Lee is only 17, and after having had a few games with Manchester United juniors last season he applied to Everton for trials. He has proved an outstanding success, and no doubt Secretary Mr Theo Kelly will ensure that Scott-Lee is not allowed to leave Merseyside, as was Soo, who went from Liverpool schoolboys circles to Prescot and then on to Stoke."

The *Daily Worker*, always among Frank's biggest supporters, was equally impressed, although their comments might seem a little bit patronizing to the twenty-first century reader:

CHINESE BRILLIANCE FOR EVERTON

J. Scott-Lee is a Chinese, and a graduate at Liverpool University. He is also a smashing little footballer. He made his debut at wing-half for Everton against Burnley on Saturday and gave a splendid account of himself. When Everton saw him play for Manchester United some time ago, they at once saw him to be a player of potential class. He is cool and has stamina. Scott-Lee knows that, as a half-back his job is to supply the ball to the men in front.

According to experts who have seen football played in China, the Chinese excel at the British winter game. Our lads have to play on the highest note to beat the Orientals. Frank Soo, Stoke and England half-back, who is half-Chinese, suggests by his brilliance that there is something about the Chinese that makes him a good soccer player.

Frank was making fewer appearances for Stoke City. In the 1942/43 season he only played for them twelve times, scoring three goals including a penalty in City's 5-2 defeat of Derby County on 26 September 1942. It was Stoke's third penalty of the match, the previous two having been missed. On 21 November he played for the RAF at the Victoria Ground, along with Matthews in a fundraising match against an FA XI. The Butler Street Stand was opened to accommodate the crowd of 23,500. The FA XI won 4-3 but the highlight for many Stoke supporters would have been Soo's goal when he headed in a Matthews' corner. The crowd, it was reported, was "set alight" by the interaction between their two heroes. The match raised £2,214 for RAF charities.

Frank's last game in the league for Stoke City the 1942/43 season was at the Victoria Ground against Wrexham on 28 November. After that he was either injured or unavailable. Tommy Sale, himself coming back from an injury, replaced him at left-half. On 19 December 1942 Frank was transferred to 15 (Pilot) Advanced Flying Unit, which was somewhere "in the south of England," probably at Greenham Common in Berkshire. 15 PAFU, like his other units was involved in the training of pilots of Oxford aircraft in the use of the Beam Approach system. Frank's postings were taking him further and further away from Stoke and he began to make more guest appearances for clubs in the London area. This included playing for Chelsea, Reading and Brentford.

McGrory decided that with Frank's increasing unavailability for Stoke that he would remove the captaincy for the 1943/44 season, handing the honour to Tommy Sale. Frank would spend the remainder of the war quite a distance away from Stoke-on-Trent, moving in turn to RAF Feltwell, RAF Croughton, RAF Bovingdon in Hertfordshire and RAF Ternhill in Shropshire, before ending his service career at the demobilization unit at RAF Cardington. He would finally leave the Royal Air Force in April 1946.

Frank made his first appearance for Chelsea against Southampton at Stamford Bridge on 23 January 1943, a game which Chelsea won by three goals to one. The day before he had played for an RAF XI versus an FA XI at Ashton Gate in aid of war charities. The war was taking priority over everyone's lives and Frank was no exception. On 28 July 1943 he was promoted to the rank of Leading Aircraftman, the highest rank that he would achieve during his RAF service. In the following season, 1943/44, he would only play one league and one cup match for Stoke City.

Frank was not the only member of the Soo family to make a contribution to the Allied war effort. All five brothers served in the armed forces during the war. His brother Harold was one of three RAF members of a bomber crew operating out of Norfolk, alongside four Australians. He was a mid-upper Gunner, of the rank of Sergeant in 149 Squadron. Flight-Sergeant Ronald Soo was a volunteer Air Gunner in 166 Squadron. Kenneth, who was only eight years old when war broke out, was a cadet in the RAF and Frank's future brother-in-law, Leong Kwong Chee, a Singaporean, who married Phyllis in November 1943, had also served in the RAF. Even the marriage of Frank's sister would make the pages of the Liverpool newspapers:

> Leong Kwong Chee, a 20-year-old Malayan-Chinese, of Singapore was studying aerial surveying at Singapore when war started. He came to England and joined the RAF as a photographer. On one of his 'leaves' at Liverpool he met Miss Beatrice Phyllis Soo, sister of the Stoke City and England international football, Frank Soo, of Allington-street, Aigburth. They will be married at St Michael-in-the-Hamlet church, Aigburth, on Nov. 6. Leong was released from the RAF in February this year in order to take up work as an interpreter.

Despite not being able to play for his club, Soo's stock was rising elsewhere and he was called up for more wartime internationals. On 25 September 1943, he and Stan Matthews played in an 8-3 thrashing of Wales at Wembley in front of 80,000 spectators. He was not only playing alongside footballers of the quality of Matthews but also with the likes of Denis Compton, Stan Cullis, Raich Carter and Stan Mortensen (who actually came on for Wales as a substitute when Ivor Powell broke his collar bone). Despite the fact that, as for many players of the same age, his career as a professional footballer was being swallowed up by the war, Frank must have felt that his prospects were excellent. He was given the captaincy of the RAF XI that took on a Scottish representative team at Hampden Park on 6 November. Although still subject to the by now almost-traditional comments about his ancestry - the *Daily Worker* called him "Stoke City's splendid little footballer of Chinese descent," he was increasingly also described in terms of his football achievements, as a Stoke City, RAF and England international. The *Daily Herald* regarded his appointment as captain of the RAF as a breakthrough:

FRANK SOO'S SHARE IN RAF SOCCER WIN

It has taken a war to break down football prejudice and custom. A remarkable example occurred on Saturday at Hampden Park, Glasgow. Frank Soo, Stoke City wing half-back of Chinese descent, who began his career brilliantly, led RAF on to the famous enclosure before 53,371 people and came off it proud in the captaincy of another conquest over Scotland. It was fine RAF gesture. Soo, who has played twice for England against Wales, most probably would never have been chosen by the FA in peace-time, despite all his outstanding ability. He was one of the best players on view in this RAF success, which registered Scotland's fourth consecutive defeat.

On New Year's Day 1944, Frank made a rare appearance at the Victoria Ground for a match against Wolves. It turned out to be a remarkable game in which Stoke replied to an early Billy Wright goal for the visitors with six goals in the first half. Wearing a number four shirt, Soo contributed to an eventual 9-3 scoreline. Although he did not score himself, he assisted Liddle, Sale and Freddie Steele - who scored six, "three with his head and three with his right foot" - to what was a sensational victory.

Soon afterwards Frank would have some devastating news from his family. On 14 January 1944, Frank's younger brother, Flight Sergeant Ronald Soo, aged only 23, was killed when his aircraft, an Avro Lancaster EE137, crashed during a raid on Brunswick in Germany. He had been an air gunner and navigator with a crew that were all killed in the crash. They were buried together in Hanover War Cemetery. Thirty-eight bombers went missing in what was the heaviest bombing of Germany so far following Bomber Command's decision to start a campaign of saturation bombing of key cities. It is not clear how long it took for the authorities to ascertain the identity of the air crew who died - the story only made the newspapers two months later - but the Soo family must have assumed the worst. Ronald had also been a talented schoolboy footballer and may have had a professional career similar to his brother but for the war. However badly affected his playing career was by the interruption of the war, Frank must have been all too aware that things could have been far worse.

It's impossible to know how badly affected Frank was by the death of his brother. Like everyone else, he simply had to get on with making his contribution to the war in whatever way he was asked to. In his case, this was in the form of playing for England, and on 22 April 1944, he was chosen for the national side to play Scotland at Hampden Park. The crowd of 133,000 was the largest wartime gate in the British Isles of the entire war. Frank Butler of the *Daily Express* called this team "England's best since 1907." Despite this, Frank was overlooked for the international against Wales in September 1944. Many sports journalists expressed their astonishment that his replacement Donald Welsh, of Charlton Athletic, described as "ineffective" among other things (the England halves in general were described as "a sorry lot" by the *Daily Worker*) should have been preferred.

The war in Europe was going well for the Allies and in September 1944, as the British forces reached the Rhine, the Football Association was invited by the military authorities and the football associations of France and Belgium to send a representative side to play in those countries. Footballers were drawn from the Army and RAF sides to form an FA Services XI. The fourteen players who were selected included the stalwarts, Matt Busby, Joe Mercer, Stanley Matthews, Horatio Carter and Maurice Edelston. On 30 September they played a France XI at the Parc des Princes in Paris in front of 30,000 spectators. The newly-liberated country was not to be spared on the football field. The FA Services XI won 5-0 with three goals by Raich Carter and one each from Ted Drake and Maurice Edelston. A slightly chilling reminder of what the victorious Allies were celebrating was recalled by Joe Mercer in his book, *The Great Ones:* "My wartime service took me all over the country and, after D-Day, back to the continent. In 1944 I played for the FA services against France in the first International since the liberation of Paris. It was played in the Parc des Princes stadium surrounded by a barbed wire fence which had been left by the Germans who had used the stadium as a prison camp."

Frank also played in the game against Belgium at the Stade du Daring Club de Bruxelles on 1 October. This time the crowd was 28,000 strong and the British side won by three goals (scored by Ted Drake, Walley Barnes plus an own goal) to nil. Back in England for the 1944/45 season, Frank returned to play in the League South for Brentford for which he won plaudits in the national press. Robin Baily's match report of Brentford's 4-0 away victory over Charlton Athletic in the *People* makes it sound as if Frank was at the peak of his game at this time: "It was one of those games that continually give the impression one side has four or five more players on the field than their opponents. And unfailing proof that the team which looks more numerous is a cohesive, well balanced force, while their foes are so many disconnected individuals. Some think that masterly triangular tactics have been killed by the new offside rule. They would have revelled in the smooth, complete understanding and incisive attacks of Frank Soo, Stoke's consummate half-back … the first of the four [goals] was an oil painting. Soo slipped across a perfect pass in pace and placement. Boulter ran onto it, halted in mid-stride and, half turning, delivered a right hook good enough for Jack Dempsey himself."

Frank, who had also played in another wartime international for England in a 6-2 thrashing of Scotland at Wembley on 14 October 1944, was the man of the moment and seems to have now also become something of a spokesman for professional footballers. He was certainly the go-to player for the *Daily Worker* and their interview with him, published on 4 November 1944, about proposals to pay players only £4 a week when the war was over, shows something of the forthrightness of his views:

> League and international soccer stars are becoming more and more indignant at the treatment which the football bosses are handing out, particularly at the proposal in the first post-war season to pay players £4 a match.
>
> 'It's ridiculous,' said Frank Soo, Stoke City captain and England international right-half, when I asked him about it. 'If that's what they are going to pay us, I'm leaving football and I think many other players will, too. Four pounds a match isn't a living wage for the men who devote all their time to the game. As for the rest of the club players, it will mean starvation. Only 14 players will be paid £4 every time they are selected to play. But there are anything from 30 to 35 players in a club, so what are the rest going to live on? If the proposal is carried through it will practically kill big football. How can managers encourage promising lads to take up the game when they cannot offer them a living wage? Most clubs have done well in wartime football. It's not that they couldn't afford to pay us full wages once we resumed peacetime football.
>
> 'I think that clubs must pay a minimum rate of £5 a week, with a flat rate of £10 or £12 after the player has proved his worth for a couple of seasons.'

Although he remained in England for some years after the war was over, it is interesting that when Soo had moved to Scandinavia, he would cite the attitudes of people involved in English football as among the reasons he decided to leave. He would become increasingly disenchanted with the way that English football was run and frustrated about how the small businessmen and local aldermen who were the directors of many clubs refused to reward the talented players who were after all most responsible for bringing in the paying spectators. Frank wasn't in football for the money, but he believed very strongly that players should be justly rewarded for what they contributed to the game. The maximum wage would not be abolished in England until 1961.

Back at Brentford, Frank was still winning the admiration of the *People*'s Robin Baily, who described his performance against Crystal Palace (Brentford lost 2-1 at home) in November fulsomely: "Frank Soo stood out boldly in Brentford's key department. The polished precision of his passes was alone worth the price of admission to a lover of fine football." Despite his form at club level, and his having become indispensable to the defence of the RAF touring side, he appears to have been losing ground when it came to England selection. In January 1944, the *Daily Express* suggested that his Stoke City comrade Neil Franklin should take his place, as did Frank's fans at the *Daily Worker*: "Franklin played well enough at right-half to oust his club-mate, Frank Soo, of Stoke, from the England side. The youngster proved himself an able wing-half, with the spirit of attack strong in him." Nevertheless Frank was picked to play in the international match at Villa Park on 3 February, as was Franklin. Whatever their rivalry on the pitch, Neil Franklin was one of the most generous of all Frank's contemporaries, speaking highly of him as a footballer, teammate and friend in his autobiography. Remembering his England debut, he wrote: "Not only was this a great day for me, it was also a great day for Stoke City, for besides me they had two other representatives in the England team - Frank Soo and the inevitable Stanley Matthews. ... I met the other members of the England team on the Friday before the match at the Grand Hotel, Birmingham, and Stan Matthews and Frank Soo immediately took charge of me so that I would not feel too nervous."

Later the same month Frank was moved to 5 (Pilot) Advanced Flying Unit at RAF Ternhill. The camp was in Shropshire but it was only about twenty miles from both Freda and the Victoria Ground. Frank was coming home even if he had to remain in uniform for some time to come, but his reception at Stoke City would not be a happy one. Rapturously welcomed back by many Stoke supporters, his loyalty to McGrory in the early years of the war was rewarded with being made to feel that he was surplus to requirements. His favourite number six shirt had been taken by Frank Mountford, a player that Bob McGrory had brought through himself, who had none of the "star quality" that the manager resented. Despite being a current international, it was Soo who was asked to switch positions and fill in where there were gaps. Frank continued to be co-operative and committed to the Potters' cause. He persuaded several of his RAF and England colleagues, George Hardwick (Middlesbrough), Robert Brown (Charlton Athletic) and Leslie Smith (Brentford) to offer to play for Stoke who were still very short of players, a situation that was exacerbated by the absence of Matthews because of his father's illness and subsequent death. McGrory was losing more and more of his stars to RAF and international sides too, and it clearly irritated him. His frustration led to him writing to the chairman of the FA, Stanley Rous, asking if he could be left one of Soo, Matthews and Franklin, when they were picked to go on a five day tour of Belgium in March 1945. Soo went on the tour, but was not picked to play in any of the matches, which must have added to McGrory's chagrin. There seems to have been an impasse between player and manager. McGrory wanted Frank to be available, but was not prepared to give him back a regular place in the side. Frank was now an England international and a nationally-known star. If he wasn't able to make the Stoke City team as a first choice player, how long would the England selectors remain interested in him? Rumours began circulating that he was unhappy and that his former manager, Tom Mather, was interested in signing him for Leicester City. As if to confirm his worries, Frank was dropped from the FA representative side fuelling speculation that he would not be picked for the next home international which proved to be groundless.

On 7 April 1945, Stoke lost to Manchester United in a humiliating League Cup defeat. The scoreline of 6-1, which included a Stoke own goal, was the result of having to field a team with only nine fit players. In a reversal of affairs in the early part of the war, Matthews played despite having an ankle injury and against medical advice. It was reported that Soo was not fit to play, but he appeared for England at Hampden Park only seven days later. City lost by ten goals to two over the two legs of their cup ties with Manchester United, and it is difficult to imagine that McGrory was anything other than furious with Frank. Things had come to a head and, on 10 April 1945, Frank submitted a transfer request. He was no longer prepared to play out of position. The announcement that Bob McGrory had signed a new five-year contract meant that there was little hope for Soo that the situation would change. The Stoke City board invited Frank to meet them and "air his grievances," but he declined. He had had enough. The local press, and many fans, were shocked by Frank's transfer request. Six supporters wrote to the *Sentinel*, "We do not think the treatment meted out to this player is in accordance with the services he has rendered to the club. We trust the difficulties will be overcome and that we shall see the player filling his rightful position, right-half, and in this we feel that we are by no means alone."

It was not to be. Despite Soo's undoubted popularity with fans and his international status, he was now thirty-one years old. His replacement, Frank Mountford, was only twenty-two, had lots of potential and scored goals for City regularly. If there was one criticism that could be made of Frank Soo as a player, it was that he didn't score many goals, although sadly statisticians haven't kept records of how many goals he assisted.

The dispute between Frank Soo and Stoke City was even covered in the Swedish national press. Frank was beginning to spend his summers in Scandinavia, coaching in Finland, Sweden and Denmark. It was something he would do every year until he eventually moved to Sweden permanently. Over the years he built up considerable connections with people in European football and, even in 1945, he was already featuring in Swedish newspapers like *Expressen* and *Dags Nyheter*. The British media were also taken with the story of Frank's falling-out with Stoke City. The *Western Morning News*, *Yorkshire Post* and *Hull Daily Mail*, among others, all covered the story. On 12 April the *Dundee Courier* announced that his transfer request was a "BOMBSHELL FOR STOKE CITY," echoing headlines from the days when Stanley Matthews fell out with the club in the 1930s. The *Liverpool Daily Post* reported: "Something of a minor football sensation has been caused by the announcement that Frank Soo, captain of Stoke City and England's right-half, has asked his club to place him on the transfer list because they have been playing him at inside forward. Though Soo may not regard inside forward as his best position, he is an extremely talented and skillful player who can do well anywhere. Actually he was an inside forward before Stoke converted him into a half-back, had several games there after becoming a half-back and just before the war was experimented with as a centre forward. Three years ago he played two brilliant games as a guest with Everton at inside left, getting two goals each time."

There was much discussion of the merits of Frank's case, many commentators feeling that his versatility should be regarded as a positive point and questioning why he was suddenly objecting to being played in positions he had been happy to fill throughout his time at Stoke. "The club will not say at the moment where he will play at the weekend," one newspaper reported, and readers were able to continue the debate over their Sunday breakfasts after reading an opinion piece in the *People*: "Frank Soo, Stoke's international wing-half of Chinese descent, and skipper of the team, is at loggerheads with the club and has asked to be placed on the transfer list. A most interesting issue is raised of the 'what would you do chums?' type, for, although Soo says there are other things, his chief complaint is that the club will insist on playing him in the forward line, although the England selectors think he is the best right-half in the country. I can visualise a 50-50 argument from you fans, for, while Soo is justifiably incensed because there is always the danger of him losing his touch as a great half-back and developing into just an ordinary inside forward, there is also the club's point of view. If they engage a player as a professional, are they entitled to play him when and where they like? Admirer as I am of this steady, popular Stoke star, I must say that I think the scales are rather balanced against him. You see, when he was engaged in 1935 [actually, 1932] from the Prescot Cables Liverpool club, it was as a forward. Only later, in an emergency, was he converted to half-back, so he has the Stoke club to thank for that much."

Whatever the merits of this argument, a key point here is that many of the reports mention that the dispute about where Frank played was only the main complaint that he had. He had indeed appeared to play happily as a forward, although he was getting older and so it seems counterintuitive to have asked him to move from defensive midfield to become an attacking player at the age of thirty-one. His other grievances against the club were not reported, but it is evident that Bob McGrory was an unsentimental man, who fell out with many of his best players over time. As often happens in football, both player and manager appear to have reached a point of no going back. McGrory had his replacement. Frank could only have felt a future playing in the Stoke City reserves was hardly going to benefit his remaining international career. There was no possibility of compromise.

Frank's problems in football were set in the contrasting atmosphere of a country that was celebrating the victory in Europe. Between 12 and 19 May, he, Franklin and Matthews toured Scotland with an FA team which also included Bill Shankly, Jock Dodds and Stan Mortensen, and despite his fears, Frank was still being selected for internationals. The England players celebrated VE Day in a London hotel, where they saw what Frank's Stoke teammate Neil Franklin described as the first floodlights to be switched on after six years of the blackout. During the summer break, Frank went on a tour of Switzerland. It was the Swiss FA's fiftieth anniversary and he participated in an unofficial international in Berne, which England lost, but he did not play in the 0-3 win at the Grasshoppers' Stadium in Zurich. These teams appear to have been retrospectively classified as "services XIs" by the FA, although all the players were English and they wore the official England shirt.

Frank Soo would neither be the first nor the last player at Stoke City to fall out with Bob McGrory. Matthews had a difficult relationship with his manager from the beginning and later, another star, Neil Franklin would have similar problems. Peter Buxton, a local reporter would say that: "McGrory tended to lose the plot when internationals like Stan Matthews and Neil Franklin asserted their independence." Frank was, and would always be, unafraid to stand up for himself and others. This must have been a red rag to McGrory, who appeared to set no store by what contribution a player had made to the club's success. As with Matthews, once Frank questioned McGrory's authority, he was as good as banished.

The saga of Frank's possible transfer continued over the summer of 1945. The *People* continued to report:

> My little piece about Frank Soo severing his connection with
> Stoke was responsible for another big section of my mail-bag.

Soo seems to be a great favourite in the Potteries, and quite a few people have written to say so. Here is Mr J. Penlington of Stoke-on-Trent: 'Your paragraph on Frank Soo would be read with interest by a lot of people in Stoke-on-Trent. Whether they will agree with your statement that the scales are balanced against Soo is another matter. Having engaged a player, is the club entitled to play him in any position they wish? This question may best be answered by asking what would happen if Manchester City played Frank Swift in the centre forward position or Everton and Sunderland played Tommy Lawton and Horatio Carter goal[keeper] and full-back respectively. The England selectors think Soo the best right-half in the country, and surely the player is reasonable in expecting his club to play him in the same position. As regards his engagement as an inside forward, it is interesting to note that Soo first played for Stoke in a Central League match at the Victoria Ground and occupied the left-half position.'

And here are a few comments from another Stoke epistle: 'Your information about Soo is wrong. He came as a left-half and played his first game in that position against Liverpool reserves. On the coming of Kirton he went over to the right-half position, where he gained, as you know, his international honours. For your information, Soo has 90 per cent of the supporters behind him.'

Back in Stoke-on-Trent, McGrory was still making statements about his preference for young, local players. Although he brought Stan Matthews back, the war had seen the Wizard loosen his ties with his home town. He liked living in Blackpool, had bought a hotel there, and thought it was a good place both to develop his career and to bring up his young family. Despite the prevailing view that footballers should be given contracts back at their pre-war clubs, Stoke City treated several players, including Tommy Sale and Harry Brigham quite shabbily. Worse was their treatment of goalkeeper Norman Wilkinson. He had served with the army in France and also returned to his native County Durham to work as a coal miner. During the war he had incurred a facial injury and lost a lot of weight. At thirty-five years old, he did not look like an athlete any longer. The Stoke City board's attitude was to privately express the desire to "get Wilkinson off our books at a reasonable figure."

Soo continued to feel aggrieved by his treatment. In September 1945 he finally met with the Stoke City board, telling them that going on to the transfer list would be in "the best interests of himself and the club." The directors asked him to reconsider, believing his reasons for leaving were "unfounded." To add to an already difficult situation, former Stoke

City manager and the man who had brought Frank to the Potteries, Tom Mather, now at Leicester City, asked if Frank could play as a guest, if he couldn't have him permanently. Port Vale also, rather cheekily, put in a bid for his services too. Not only did the Stoke board refuse permission, they sent their England international to play for Shrewsbury Town, who played in the Midland League, ostensibly to maintain his match fitness. This could only have seemed - to Frank as well as to everyone else - like a punishment and an attempt to humiliate him. "The Stoke directors have banned me from playing for any other League club," Soo told the press. "It is not playing the game that I should be compelled to play for a non-league club. An international, to keep his form, must play regularly in top-class football. I have not been allowed to play for any other League club since last season."

On 22 July 1945 Tom Morgan reported in the *People*: "A rumour that Stanley Matthews, the England star, is to leave Stoke City persists despite a statement by Mr Booth, the chairman, that he knew nothing about such reports. In such circumstances it is difficult to obtain a genuine denial or confirmation, but all I can say is that there is seldom smoke without fire. What I do know is that Stoke could bag the biggest fee ever paid for a footballer eclipsing that famous £14,000 paid by Arsenal to Wolves for Bryn Jones. And if Matthews did leave Stoke his new home would not be a thousand miles from Highbury, or wherever it is Arsenal play these days! Don't forget, too, that Frank Soo, the Stoke and international half-back, had a spot of bother a while back, about which I told you. That blew over, but these things do happen. I don't say anything is wrong between Matthews and Stoke, but what I do know is that Stanley is an ambitious young man anxious to make the best of a professional footballer's brief hour of glory."

By mid-August 1945, Tom Mather made his interest in Soo official and approached Stoke City regarding the transfer of Frank Soo, the international half-back. The fee was rumoured to be between £7,000 and £8,000. Frank renewed his transfer request. "I have been trying unsuccessfully since last May to get the directors to consider my request for a transfer," he said. "I am unhappy and unsettled at Stoke. I shall be sorry to leave after thirteen years, but it is best for both that we should part." He publicly expressed his wish to join Leicester City. On 5 September the Stoke City directors issued a statement to the effect that Frank Soo's concerns had been listened to and that they had given him a further opportunity of considering the matter. Soo was present at the meeting, lasting over two hours, which took place immediately before this statement was made. Three days later, presumably having had their answer from Frank, they finally acceded to his request and put him on the transfer list. It was a national story. The *Sunday Mirror* reported on 9 September: "The Frank Soo transfer story is almost over. Stoke yesterday put him on the transfer list. The Stoke chairman said he thought Frank's reasons for wanting to move were not really adequate, but the club would not stand in his way if he was determined to go. The best bet in football is that Frank will rejoin his old chief, Tom Mather, at Leicester - or are Chelsea nibbling at this one, too?"

On 15 September, Soo joined his England teammates and travelled to Belfast to play in a Victory International against Ireland at Windsor Park. On the journey, their train had been derailed at Lambrigg, near Kendal in Cumberland, but none of the party was injured. Stanley Matthews described the incident in one of his autobiographies: "Travelling with me were Frank Swift, Joe Mercer, Frank Soo, Neil Franklin, Bill Watson and Raich Carter, but we were all sleeping and knew nothing of the incident until we arrived at Stranraer many hours late. The rest of the party, travelling from London, were relieved to know we were safe, and were a little disappointed when we could not relate any details of the mishap. While we slept we we had been shunted onto a siding, blissfully unaware of what might have been a sticky business." The match, which attracted 45,061 people, ended with a 1-0 win for England, the only goal being scored by Stan Mortensen. The *Daily Worker* said that Soo was "on top form."

Newspaper reports claimed that Tom Mather had placed a bid of £5,000 for Frank, which was echoed by a similar claim from the Port Vale board, but Stoke's chairman, Harry Booth, rejected them both. "The offer does not reach our minimum figure," Booth told the *Daily Express*. "But the matter is open to negotiation. Stoke directors want to see Soo settle down again in football, and where ever he goes it will be with our blessing." It was also reported that Newcastle United, Manchester City, and Blackpool were interested and bids of around £4,500 were coming in for him. On 26 September 1945, a few days after he had scored a goal for Shrewsbury Town in the Midland League, Stoke City finally agreed to sell Frank Soo to Leicester City for £4,600 and on 27 September 1945, he left the Potteries and the football club he would many years later say he never wanted to leave.

Town Row in the early twentieth century. The Royal Oak is in the foreground and the building beyond it was already a Chinese laundry.

West Derby Infants' School in 1926. It's likely that all seven of the Soo children attended this school.

The West Derby Boys Club football team 1930/31. Frank was alread winning trophies.

Frank Soo at Stoke City, cutting a dash whether on or off duty.

(Pictures courtesy of Staffordshire Sentinel News & Media)

Stoke City 1939. Bob McGrory is standing second left and Stanley Matthews is seated, far left on the front row.

(Photograph courtesy of Neville Evans)

Frank and Freda's wedding in Stoke-on-Trent. Quan and Beatrice are on the right, the bridesmaid is Frank's sister, Phyllis and the small boy is his youngest brother, Kenny.

(Photograph courtesy of Christian Hill)

Frank is presented to General Koening, representing the French government, on 26 May 1945 at Wembley Stadium in front of 65,000 spectators.

(Photograph courtesy of John Soo)

Ronnie Soo dressed for duty as part of air crew and for football, not long before his death in 1944.

(Photographs courtesy of Jacqui Soo)

The Royal Air Force team arrive in Lisbon for a friendly in 1946.
(Photograph from Neil Franklin's scrapbook supplied by Neville Evans)

The teams line up before the start of a match against the Portuguese Army.
(Neville Evans)

Luton Town, circa 1947
(Photograph courtesy of John Soo)

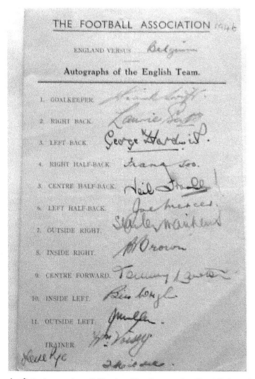

Left Autographs of England's players for the Victory International against Belgium in 1946.
Frank dropped out at the last minute. (Courtesy of Neville Evans) *Right* Quan & Beatrice's grave.
(Jacqui Soo)

4

'THE MAN OF THE MOMENT'
Leicester, Luton, Chelmsford, 1945 - 1950

Frank Soo's move from Stoke City to Leicester was not made in ideal circumstances, but it must have seemed like a good move to him at the time. He strongly believed that he had a good few years ahead of him as a player. He was extremely fit and rarely suffered from health problems or injuries. The time he had spent coaching in Scandinavia every summer for the last few years had given him the ideal grounding to translate his playing skills into the training of other footballers, but it's unlikely that Frank felt that it was anything like time to give up playing the game competitively. There was no reason why he wouldn't have expected to carry on being picked for England either, now that the war was over. Leicester was a good move from his personal point of view too, not very far from Freda's family in North Staffordshire. Neither was it far from RAF Tern Hill, where he was still stationed, although with hostilities at an end it was only a matter of time until his demobilization. Although he was sorry to leave Stoke, the time had come for him to move on. Frank was still a popular and well-liked player. His argument had been only with his manager and the club's directors. The sympathies of the majority of the public and the press were with the player during his row with McGrory as this item from the *Sunday Mirror* of 27 September 1945 demonstrates:

> At last Frank Soo will be able to play with a load off his mind. Leicester City announced yesterday that this player had been transferred to their books and will play for them against Plymouth at Leicester on Saturday. Thus ends a long-drawn-out tussle between this international player and Stoke City, for whom he had played for twelve years. Soo had been at loggerheads with the Stoke officials since last season on the simple matter of his playing position. As he knew that he could not do his best in such circumstances, Soo asked for his transfer, which has been withheld until now. This buying and selling of players remains a blot on professional football. Many otherwise brilliant performers are playing below their form merely because they are forced by the system to stay where

they are unhappy. In the case of Soo he has been prevented from playing League football since last season because his club held fast to the figure they had set upon him as transfer fee. In going to Leicester City Soo renews acquaintance with the manager who gave him his start in League football.

The Football League did not return to its old structure for another season and Leicester City were in League South, along with several of the clubs that Soo had served as a guest player during the war: Chelsea, Brentford and Millwall. Tom Mather clearly had plans for the club and brought in a number of new players plus guest players like the talented striker Emilio Aldecoa, who had come to Britain as a boy, a Basque refugee from the Spanish Civil War. The team also included a young Don Revie, the future manager of England. If Soo was somewhat older than the player that Mather had left behind at Stoke in 1935, he still felt that Frank had the qualities that were needed to lead the team to success, but it was not to be. In his debut game against Plymouth Argyle at Filbert Street on 29 September, Leicester scraped a draw. Around 24,000 (estimates vary) Leicester supporters - double the usual number - turned up to see the new signing. "Surely," asked the *Daily Express* football correspondent, "All this is in favour of the argument that a player is worth what he draws at the box office?" But, according to the *Western Morning Press*, the fans were to be disappointed with their first view of the new £5,000 signing. He was constantly crowded out by the Argyle defenders and he was able to contribute very little to what was a below par Leicester performance. The *Leicester Mercury* was much more complimentary to Soo however: "Soo was soon prominent in a delightful bit of work in concert with Danny Liddle and Aldecoa, which led to Dyer clearing under difficulties from his goalmouth." Along with Sep Smith, Frank opened up many penetrating attacks with his accurate passing. In the second half Mather swapped Smith and Soo over, Frank going to the right flank. He narrowly missed scoring when the Argyle goalkeeper, Shortt, saved his header from under the bar and almost had a late winner for Leicester six minutes from time when he took a pass from Liddle and hit it against the far post where it rebounded across the goal mouth. The keeper was beaten but the ball didn't go into the net.

It was not long - on 6 October - until Soo was made team captain. It's possible that Mather had discussed the captaincy with Frank in his efforts to attract him to his club, although Sep Smith, thought to be approaching retirement, was a popular and effective skipper. Smith, who spent his entire professional career at Filbert Street, was a father figure and mentor to many of the younger players. Don Revie devoted an entire chapter of his autobiography to him. It was called "What I Owe To Sep Smith." There were no reports of dissent, but it's hard to believe it didn't rankle a little bit with some of the more established players. Smith played in the game against Portsmouth at Fratton Park, which Leicester lost 2-0, when Frank took over the captain's armband. Along with Davies, Smith and Soo provided the Foxes with an all-international half-back line.

There did not seem to be any hard feelings about the captaincy and in the return fixture a week later at Filbert Street, in front of a sizeable post-war crowd of more than 18,000, Soo and Sep Smith were congratulated by James Stephens, the *Leicester Mercury* reporter, for their "brilliant constructive work" together. In fact, it was Smith's long dropping pass from the wing that enabled Frank to head the ball into the Portsmouth goal and put City into the lead in the twenty-ninth minute. It was Soo's first goal for his new club and, characteristically, he ran straight over to shake Sep Smith's hand. The game, which again featured Emilio Aldecoa as a guest player, was an exciting, hard-fought one and Smith was able to score the winning goal after Aldecoa was brought down just inside the penalty area sixteen minutes from time.

On 20 October 1945, Soo and Joe Mercer - whose connection dated back to their schoolboy football days in the north west - were playing together again, this time with Mercer as captain of England in the second Victory international at the Hawthorns. Played in front of 56,000 people, many of whom had travelled en masse from Wales, it was to be Frank's last appearance as an England player. Although Stan Matthews was celebrating what should have been his forty-third England cap - it wouldn't count, of course - which equalled Eddie Hapgood's record, most observers were now looking at these international friendlies as trial matches. Young players like Albert Stubbins (Newcastle United), Willie Watson (Huddersfield Town) and James Hagan (Sheffield United), replacing Lawton, Mortensen and Leslie Smith, were there in the hope of impressing the England selectors. In fact, only Hagan made more than one appearance for England. Despite not playing well himself in this match, Matthews would carry on playing for England until 1958. The game ended with a surprising - at least it was surprising to the English press - one-nil victory to Wales. The inevitable post-match criticism centred upon the forwards. Matthews was suffering from the absence of Raich Carter. Their partnership was vital to Matthews' goal-scoring success and it was only Soo who was able to do anything to support his former club teammate.

Because of the international, Frank missed that season's home match against Nottingham Forest but he was back for the return fixture at the City Ground on 27 October and managed to save the day by scoring an equalizer in the eighty-eighth minute, as the *Leicester Mercury* reported: "Two minutes from time Soo came over from the right and tried a long shot. Platts appeared to have the attempt covered but he let the ball slip out of his arms and into the net. It was a lucky equalizer but Leicester were quite worthy of the draw."

While Soo and his fellow internationals were playing at West Bromwich, an increasingly controversial aspect of association football was emerging: the distribution of money in the game and the unfairness of player's wages and conditions. During the England-Wales match, club directors and Football League officials met at the Hawthorns to discuss an offer which had just been made by Unity Pools, a wartime company that had been formed in 1939, following the government's prompting, by merging the three major pools companies, Littlewoods, Vernons and Zetters. To save paper, pools coupons had been printed in newspapers. Unity Pools had obviously done well out of the arrangement and was now offering the Football League £100,000 (the equivalent of four million pounds today) "for the benefit of clubs and players." The Football League was generally opposed to the idea of any association between the game and pools companies, but the directors of football clubs felt differently and proposed a compromise in which half the sum was invested in a comprehensive insurance policy which would indemnify both clubs and players against career-ending injuries. Perhaps a measure of the strength of feeling over this issue was shown by the absence of Will Cuff, then President of the Football League Management Committee, who stayed at home "to prepare his speech" on the subject. He was vehemently opposed to the idea.

There was also conflict about players' wages, which had been brewing for years. It was not only Stanley Matthews who was unhappy with earning such a miserable wage when gate receipts were increasing again after wartime restrictions had been lifted. The club boards felt that they had suffered greatly during the war, when their incomes fell dramatically and they were unwilling to share their profits more equitably with the players, but times were changing. Just as in many other walks of life, footballers had served in the armed forces, travelled, met and talked to people from all kinds of backgrounds. When the war was over, working people wanted more recognition of what they had contributed during years of hardship and deprivation and social and financial equality was high on the agenda. A General Election in the summer of 1945 would see Winston Churchill's government swept out of office and a landslide victory for Labour. The disputes in football reflected this change of mood and in November 1945, the *Daily Worker* reported that footballers, through the Players' Union, had voted to go on strike, the newspaper's main concern being that it might affect the forthcoming tour of Moscow Dynamo: "Whether the stoppage will extend to the matches scheduled for Moscow Dynamo – who are held up by weather conditions – remains to be seen. It seems to me that the strike will last less than a month. Never before have a small body of professional people had such support from the public as the Soccer players have today. The League is on its own in this dispute. High ranking officials of the Football Association regard the players' case as fair and sound. There is scant sympathy for the League."

Frank Soo, about to leave for Dusseldorf to captain an FA XI which was playing BAOR (the British Army of the Rhine) on 4 November, was unequivocal in his own support for the strike: "We are behind our Union all the way, and we'll win. The lads are determined not to be talked out of a decent wage. Pay is the most important issue at the moment. There are other things we consider are wrong, and we will fight to get those settled too."

The interview that Frank gave to the *Daily Worker* at this time is typical of him and he was often the player that journalists - from newspapers of all political persuasions - turned to for a view on similar issues. It suggests that he may have had some involvement with the Players' Union - the precursor of the Professional Footballers' Association - but there is no evidence that he was involved in a formal capacity and indeed he is not mentioned at all in the memoirs of the Players' Union President (and Portsmouth captain) from 1946 until 1957, Jimmy Guthrie.

The FA team's flight was delayed by fog, and the team didn't fly to Dusseldorf until the day of the game, 4 November, but the match went ahead and Soo was able to lead his team to a five-two victory over the BAOR, watched by 35,000 servicemen. On 17 November 1945, Frank was back at Filbert Street playing for Leicester City against Wolves, who deservedly won according to reports. City "lacked sparkle" and despite Soo's continuing efforts to feed the ball through to the forwards, there was little end product. The return fixture at Molineux went even more badly. "Wolves always looked like winning," according to the *Birmingham Evening Gazette*. Leicester lost by three goals to nil, although once again Frank and the stalwart Sep Smith were picked out as the players who impressed. Frank missed the away fixture against West Ham on 1 December but returned for the match against them at home on the 8th: "Leicester City took full advantage of their opportunities in the first half of their return match with West Ham at Filbert Street, although flattered by a 4-1 interval lead. Without E. Smith (injured) for most of the second-half City had to concentrate more on defence. The home side, like West Ham, got the ball into the net again, but the referee ruled against them. ... West Ham was very threatening in the first few minutes and even though Small failed to turn a shot from Whitchurch into the net with Grant out of goal, City anxiety was not at once removed, for the home goalkeeper fumbled a ball headed back to him by Soo and was lucky to get it at the second attempt. ... The opening stages found West Ham generally quicker on the ball, and apart from individual cleverness by Sep. Smith, Soo and Revie, City did not receive much encouragement, but, after 13 minutes the home side went ahead with a surprise goal."

On 12 December Frank was in another FA XI, this time against a Combined Services XI at Fratton Park. Once again it was widely regarded as a trial match. Only four of the FA side, including Soo, were already internationals. The *Daily Mirror*'s sports reporter, Armour Milne, certainly thought so: "In the unofficial England Soccer trial at Portsmouth yesterday Combined Services beat the FA XI by 4 goals to 1. But the FA selectors learned little beyond what they already knew. ... Mainly, however, it was a game in which the old brigade fully justified themselves. Brown scored for the Combined Services in the first half. Lawton twice and Mullen once in the second half. Stubbins, for the FA XI, scored late in the second half, but the credit for this goal must go to Frank Soo."

By the time they had lost by three goals to one to West Bromwich Albion at Filbert Street on 15 December, Leicester City had dropped down to seventeeth place in League South (out of 22 teams). They played Albion again on 22 December at the Hawthorns and lost once again, this time by three goals to two. Frank scored the second goal, but their opponents were dominant throughout the game and worthy winners. Given his performances so far for Leicester, there was no reason why Frank Soo should have been anything other than a popular and respected member of the squad, but Leicester were not performing at all well under Tom Mather and Filbert Street does not appear to have been a happy place in the immediate post-war period. What happened next was rather odd. Soo made the apparent mistake of playing for Port Vale in an "unsanctioned" match against Mansfield on Christmas Eve 1945 when he had returned to Stoke-on-Trent for the seasonal holiday. He was described as a "surprise guest" by the *Nottingham Evening Post* who added that "Soo's class was always in evidence, and he prompted the Port Vale right wing pair cleverly." He helped to create one of the Port Vale goals with a "brilliant" pass, but his appearance for another club did not go down at all well the directors of Leicester City Football Club.

It is difficult to understand what Frank was thinking of in playing in this match without his club's permission. Perhaps he was doing someone a favour, but even someone as football crazy as he was must have realized that it was likely to cause trouble. City had been very generous in allowing him to continue playing for England and the FA, and he had missed important fixtures for his club because of his commitments elsewhere, but the directors were undoubtedly irritated by this unauthorized appearance. The guest player system was being wound down following the end of the war and competitions like the FA Cup, and to a lesser extent the leagues, were returning to pre-war rivalries. At any rate, Frank's relationship with Leicester City appears to have deteriorated after this, despite the fact that he managed to reach St Andrew's to play for the Foxes on Christmas Day. The scoreline (Birmingham won by six goals to two) cannot have helped Frank's case. He was not dropped immediately but was moved to inside forward for the match against Spurs on 29 December 1945. The *Daily Express* was one newspaper that was puzzled by the decision: "Leicester springs a surprise by putting Frank Soo at inside forward. It will be recalled that one of the reasons Soo asked to be placed on the transfer list by Stoke was that though he was an England wing-half, the club insisted on playing him at inside forward. Tom Mather, the Leicester manager, explained the position yesterday. 'Soo realises we are not too well off for inside men, and, as captain, he has agreed to help the club out in difficult times.' Soo, a great wing half, is one of the few footballers today who really tries to play football rather than take the easier way out by ballooning the ball to the four winds. He can play anywhere."

It seems possible that moving him to a different position was a reaction to Soo's Christmas faux pas. An equally odd "coincidence" was the out-of-the-blue announcement by the Chairman of Derby County rejecting Frank's services as a player, which appeared in the *Derby Daily Telegraph* on 3 January 1946:

NOT INTERESTED IN SOO – RAMS' CHAIRMAN

'Derby County are definitely not interested in Frank Soo.'

This statement by Mr B. Robshaw, chairman of the club, made to a *Telegraph* representative today, answers rumours that the Rams are contemplating signing the Leicester City International.

Mr J. S. Catterall, secretary of Derby County, explained how the rumour started. 'The Leicester City chairman rang up Mr Robshaw and suggested that the county might be interested in buying Soo,' he said. 'They know we have just signed [Raich] Carter, and probably thought we might be prepared to spend some more money.

'It was given consideration, but we had rather a shock when we found out Soo's age.' (Soo is 33.)

Mr Catterrall denied that there had been any further negotiations with Leicester. 'The whole matter is closed as far as Derby County is concerned,' he said.

If nothing else, this was embarrassing for Soo, who prided himself on being as fit as a twenty-five year old, and had done nothing to undermine the idea that he was fit enough for his career to last for many more years. The additional news that Derby had offered Jackie Stamps in "part exchange" which was published on 7 January, also in the *Express*, probably added insult to injury.

Despite all this, Frank was back playing for City in both legs of the FA Cup third round on 5 (away) and 10 (home) January, but things went from bad to worse. Leicester managed a draw in the first game and Soo played well, at least according to the *Leicester Mercury*: "Now and again Smith or Soo flashed out with a discreet long pass to the wing... . The crowd had another big thrill... at the Chelsea end, where [Stan] Mercer accepted a beautiful pass from Soo, and shot against the foot of the near post. Robertson completely beaten. This was hard luck for Leicester." Leicester lost in a feisty replay at Stamford Bridge, by two goals to nil. Frank was injured twice in this game, wrenching his knee and receiving a nasty cut near his right eye. He was limping when Chelsea scored their first goal and had to go off later in the first half because of the cut to his eye. He came back on for the second half with a heavily bandaged knee, a plaster over his right eye and limping badly. He played well apparently, despite this, but had to switch to a place on the wing. The injuries meant that he missed some matches for City but they also put his chances of playing in the next England international in jeopardy. Newspapers reported that he was a "doubt" but he still went down to Wembley, determined to play if at all possible. The game, which would be watched by the Prime Minister, Clement Attlee, and several members of the Cabinet, plus a delegation from the United Nations, was against a Belgian side that did not include a single professional player. Several members of team had been resistance fighters during the war and the team was selected by Major M. Chome, who had been a German Prisoner of War for five years. Nevertheless, according to the *Yorkshire Post*, "the Belgians showed themselves to be fast and exceptionally fit."

Frank made every effort to play in this game, but despite the announcement by the *Daily Mirror* on 19 January that "there was never any doubt" that he was fit enough, he failed the fitness test and had to withdraw. Stanley Matthews, who very nearly didn't play himself made a rare mention of Frank in relation to this match in his first autobiography, *Feet First*, but only to say that "it was Frankie Soo who had to pull out shortly before the match owing to a twisted knee muscle. This situation gave Jesse Pye of Notts County... a chance to make his first appearance for England." This meant that young Billy Wright, who had been chosen to play at inside left, was moved to right half and take Frank's place. The replacement was ominous and, although no one knew that Frank's England career was now over, the arrival of Wright, who was young, prodigiously talented, and a future England captain, must have been a clear indication that a new generation of players was on its way. The change from a board of selectors to the appointment of an national manager, Walter Winterbottom, probably also spelt the end for many of the old guard.

Soon after this Frank hit the headlines again. On 25 January the *Daily Mirror* reported that he had been placed on Leicester's transfer list "at his own request" although some reports said that it was "by mutual agreement." It came as a shock to almost everyone. Soo had only been at the club for three months. Despite his age, it had been expected that he would be there for several seasons. City had spent a reported £5,000 on him and had clearly expected to receive more than a few months' service in return. Leicester sent a circular around to other clubs saying that they were open to offers.

What brought on such a sudden falling out? It seems unlikely to be only the unauthorized Christmas Eve game for Port Vale. There were ways of penalizing a player for that kind of breach of the rules. Neither does it seem reasonable that it was connected to City's dire results that season. If anything, Frank was the pick of the Leicester side and was often instrumental in producing the most entertaining moments of football. The fans loved him. It seems very strange that both sides appeared to want to burn their bridges quite so suddenly. In addition to this, Soo was not the only unhappy member of the squad at that time. On 8 February 1946, the *Dundee Courier* reported that Leicester City's three internationals were all on the transfer list. The Welsh international full-back, Dai Jones, Leicester City and Danny Liddle, the Scottish left-winger, were also on the list.

The reasons were never made clear, but Filbert Street was not a happy place in 1946. Not only had the team conceded twenty-four goals while scoring only eight in five league games, five players had captained the side in the space of a few weeks: Frank Soo, Sep Smith, Billy Frame, Dai Jones, and Bert Howe. In addition to this, professional footballers were still threatening to go on strike about the issue of the maximum wage. Could Soo's outspokenness on behalf of his teammates have alienated the Leicester board of directors? His willingness to give interviews with the *Daily Worker* on the subject would surely not have gone down well. Even spokesmen for the Players' Union were reluctant to talk to the Daily Worker because of its reputation as a far-left newspaper. City may have been tolerant of Soo's frequent absences to play football for England, the FA and the RAF but this tolerance would have been stretched thin if he was also part of a campaign for strike action. He had spoken publicly about his support for the Players' Union and in favour of a strike. His determination to play for England when he was not, apprently, able to turn out for Leicester because of the injuries he had received in the match against Chelsea, would not have impressed either.

Frank was listed in the team to play against Arsenal, which Leicester lost four-five, on 26 January, but did not play for City again until 23 February. In the meantime there would be plenty of demands for his services, as a player and a coach in the forthcoming close season. The Swedish newspaper *Expressen* reported that Soo would be coming to play at the Råsunda Stadium in Stockholm as part of an RAF touring team, along with former Stoke City teammates, Stanley Matthews and Neil Franklin. They were all also chosen to go to Portugal on 15 and 16 February 1946, which cannot have pleased the Leicester board of directors at all.

Although a "friendly," the RAF game in Portugal received considerable attention and live commentary was even broadcast on the BBC Light

Programme. According to Neil Franklin in his autobiography, *Soccer at Home and Abroad*, the RAF fielded a side "of tremendous strength: Williams (Wolverhampton Wanderers); Scott (Arsenal), Barker (Huddersfield Town); Soo (Stoke City), Franklin (Stoke City), Paterson (Glasgow Celtic); Matthews (Stoke City), Dougall (Birmingham City), Fenton (Middlesbrough), Brown (Charlton Athletic), Smith (Aston Villa). Even so, we only managed to draw 1-1."

According to Franklin, the RAF were faced with opponents from the Portuguese army, "but the Portuguese were afraid they could not field a strong enough team to beat us, so they craftily called up some of the reservists! These reservists were ace footballers who went into a special training spell of fourteen days' duration!"

Franklin also claimed that black market tickets for the game at the Estadio Nacional were changing hands at fifteen times the normal price, similar to the amount people were willing to pay to get into Wembley Stadium for the FA Cup Final. Whatever the cost, 80,000 people paid to see Stanley Matthews and the eight other England internationals perform.

Frank continued to play for the RAF - he had not yet been "demobbed," so he would not have had a choice in the matter - and was picked for the team to play against the Army at Stamford Bridge on 13 March and the Royal Navy at Villa Park on 3 April. In the middle of this, another shock awaited him at Filbert Street when Tom Mather resigned as manager after only nine months in the job. It was immediately announced that former Leicester City player John Duncan would be taking over. No real explanation was given for Mather's sudden departure, although the *Daily Express* stated that "There was a difference between the board and himself regarding... policy." This rather meaningless statement probably covers a number of disagreements between the manager, the players and the directors of the club. Dave Smith and Paul Taylor, authors of the definitive club history, *Of Fossils and Foxes*, say that Mather never picked a team during his time there, a seemingly bizarre state of affairs considering that acquiring good players and team selection were regarded as his strengths as a football manager. As Frank had doubtless been attracted to sign for Leicester by the prospect of working with Mather again, this would have been the point of no return for him as far as the club was concerned, although it's unlikely that he would have stayed even if Mather had.

Frank's fame was still such that his demobilization on 26 April 1946 was announced in the press, along with that of Tommy Lawton from the Army. He was officially discharged from the services at 102 Personnel Dispatch Centre, RAF Cardington, but would remain as a Class G reserve until 30 June 1959. To all intents and purposes, however, Frank Soo's air force career was over and he was free to go where he wanted to when he wanted to. The following day he turned out as a guest player for Burnley at Turf Moor. It was not the first time he had played for them, but this appearance may have been something of a trial match as his situation at Leicester was well known. In May, as part of the RAF tour of Scandinavia, Soo made an impression on the Swedish press. He was already making a name for himself and building up a network of contacts by coaching in Scandinavia every summer. Whether it was because he was becoming well-known there or not, the Swedish press regarded Frank as the pick of the RAF side, along with Stan Mortensen. They were both "noted for good shots," according to the *Dagens Nyheter*, who also described Soo as "a brilliant player, as well in defence as in attack." His reception in Sweden must have contrasted sharply with the problems he was having back at Filbert Street. Despite all the negative publicity surrounding his request for a transfer, he was one of only two Leicester City players to be on the club's retained list over the summer, the other being Stan Mercer. He didn't sign a new contract, however. A quietly determined man, Frank never wavered once he had made the decision that it was time to move on. Fiercely loyal and dedicated to every cause he was asked to support, he was disappointed when he didn't receive the same loyalty and commitment in return.

On 27 June 1946, the *Daily Express* announced the reason why Soo had failed to sign for Leicester:

SOO WILL SIGN FOR LUTON

Frank Soo, only footballer of Chinese extraction ever to play for England, is to be transferred from Leicester City to Luton Town today.

Soo is a brilliant player either at wing half or inside forward. He prefers to play at half back. He cost Leicester £5,000, and Luton are to pay the highest fee in their history to secure his services.

Leicester City had played the 1945/46 season in League South, the league structure having retained its wartime configuration for a final season. The return to post-war normality in 1946/47 saw them playing in Division Two, so moving to Luton Town, who were in the same division, must have seemed like a sensible decision. It was reported that Luton had offered Leicester City between £3,000 and £3,500 for Frank Soo, which would have been one of the highest transfer fees in the club's history, if the figure was correct. The *Leicester Mercury* reported that "Soo was in contact with [the new Leicester City] Manager John Duncan today, and was then anticipating an interview with the Luton manager, George Martin, at Stoke, preparatory to the necessary meeting between representatives of both clubs for the transfer signatures."

Soo's experience at Leicester City seems to have been unfortunate. It would not have been unreasonable for him to have assumed that he would have been treated as a respected senior player and the obvious successor to Sep Smith as team captain. Instead the captaincy was given to several players and the club was in disarray. If his decision to play one unauthorized match for another club was foolish, it seems unlikely that it would have the catalyst for a breakdown in relations between Frank and his club alone. Were there other reasons then for Frank's apparently sudden desire to leave?

Around this time, according to Frank Soo's family, a cartoon was published in the *Leicester Mercury* depicting him as a Chinese "coolie" and implying that he should not be playing for England. Despite a diligent search, it has not been possible to find this cartoon, although it was not uncommon for racism of this kind to appear in newspapers at that time. The detail of the Soo family's memory of the cartoon suggests that there is some truth in the story. If so, one can only imagine the hurt that Frank Soo must have felt. It would have been in stark contrast to all the match reports in the *Mercury* which never referred to his Chinese background during the time he spent at Leicester City. Whatever the reasons, Frank appears to have made a sudden decision to ask for a transfer and once he had made that decision he was never going to change his mind.

Frank's debut for Luton Town was against Sheffield Wednesday at Kenilworth Road on 31 August 1946. His side won by four goals to one but to describe the club's start to the season as "mixed" is something of an understatement. By mid-November they had lost eight times. Frank seems to have made a habit of arriving at a new club shortly before a change of manager, and Douglas "Dally" Duncan, a Scottish left-winger arrived from Derby County in October 1946 as player-coach. He would replace George Martin as manager in June 1947. Both Duncan and Frank Soo played in a remarkable match against Newcastle United on 30 November 1946. The match is remembered to this day by the club's supporters for the astonishing turnaround of their fortunes. Luton's form, especially at home, had picked up in the weeks leading up to this game. They had beaten Barnsley on 2 November and, even more surprisingly, Spurs on the 16th, although they lost away at Swansea on 23 November. Even the Hatter's most deluded supporters would probably not have expected much when Newcastle, top of the division, came down to Kenilworth Road with an extremely strong team that included Len Shackleton and Jackie Milburn. The occasion has gone into the area's local history and an essay about the match appears in a collection called *Legacies* by Vic Lea, which is worth quoting at length because it provides us with a rare contemporary description of Frank Soo the footballer by someone who watched him play:

> One of the greatest players ever to wear the familiar black and white rig of the 'Hatters' of Luton Town was that famous Anglo-Chinese, Frank Soo. Always popular with the crowds wherever

he went, he will be remembered particularly by Luton fans for his special brand of clever, cultured ball-play. Like most great stars, he had a characteristic touch which indicated class and it was the constant delight of all who saw it. He employed a sort of skip-pass manoeuvre which bewildered and often embarrassed opposing players. A fine club man, Frank Soo maintained a great interest in local amateurs and young players. In every respect, it was one of the astutest moves on the part of Luton town's Board of Directors when they accomplished Frank Soo's transfer. They had secured a player of international repute and vast experience.

The Luton team left the pitch at half-time three goals to nil down and, according to Hall's report, it was what went on in the dressing-room, that transformed a dejected side into match winners:

> At the interval, eleven dejected, spiritually and morally beaten Luton players left the field. Seated in the dressing room, they exchanged not so much as a word as they listened to the galling chitchat of their opponents in the neighbouring room. The 'Geordies' were on top of the world. They made up one of the finest footballing combinations in Britain at the time, and had been at their brilliant best in that first half. The guiles of Shackleton and Bentley and the speed and thrust of Wayman, Pearson and Milburn had been demoralising. Swift, devastating attacks had left the home team's defence floundering, and three goals – which might so easily have been more – pointed to the absolute nature of Newcastle's supremacy. Equally depressing was Luton's failure to so much as test the visiting goalkeeper with a worthwhile shot.

The story goes, and it appears to have come from Frank Soo, that the manager, George Martin, came into the home dressing-room unnoticed. Furious, he kicked a bucket of water so hard it flew in the air and brought all eleven players to their feet. It was, said Soo, with typical understatement, "the most unusual peptalk I have ever heard." Martin angrily told his players that he didn't expect them to be able to live with the talents that United had brought with them, but he asked them to go back out and score a single goal. He didn't mind if they let in another three, but he demanded that his players scored a goal. He then turned on his heels and left.

According to Lea, the talk "had astounding results. The team actually raced onto the field before for the restart of the game. In fact, they had all taken up their positions on the field before their rivals had left the dressing room. It was an amazing sight and the crowd, having had little to cheer about, seemed to sense their teams urgency. A profound hush settled over the entire ground as the 'Geordies' trooped to their places.

Hardly had the blast of the referees whistle died away when a roar of excitement surged from the terraces. Luton had swept into the attack, and with such fury that the hitherto immaculate defence reeled in surprise. In the opening seconds the Newcastle goalkeeper was in action, tipping a fierce, rising shot from Hugh Billington, the centre-forward, over the crossbar.

Again and again the ball bobbed and bounced dangerously about the Newcastle goal. So fierce was the pressure that the 'Geordies' were unable to clear their lines with the directness previously shown. With the shouts of their supporters ringing in the ears, the 'Hatters' attacked their rivals goal repeatedly, even the Town's full backs joining in at times.

Under such pressure, even the highly reputed Newcastle side began to panic. A hurried pass was intercepted by Luton's left half, the ball smartly slipped to Billy Waugh on the extreme left wing and carried past two defenders before being set at the foot of the 'Hatters' centre forward. Hugh Billington met it on the run and smashed it with his left foot, the ball striking the goal net with such force that it shook the rigging and rebounded onto the field.

The Hatters scored their second goal minutes later. Their right full-back took the ball off Roy Bentley, Newcastle's star striker and passed it to Billington who drove it low and hard across the Newcastle goalmouth. Billy Waugh slipped it back to Allenby Driver who kicked the ball into the top right hand corner of the net from twenty-five yards away. Inspired by the two goals, Town continued to attack and Melville Daniels, Town's inside right, was able to almost walk the ball into the net for their third. The last goal came a few minutes before the final whistle following a clever piece of work by Frank Soo who passed the ball to Hugh Billington who turned and shot. The ball flew thirty yards into the net and amazingly, Newcastle were beaten.

Frank would later recall the victory as one of his proudest moments. The victory did little to kick start the club's season, however, and they had to wait until 11 January 1947 for their next memorable game, a six-nil win over Third Division Notts County in the third round of the FA Cup. Such goal-scoring was rare that season, but Soo did not come in for criticism, indeed the Hatters were regarded as being "particularly strong at right-half." It was a very hard winter and many matches were played on snow. A hundred Luton fans travelling to watch their club play Burnley in an FA

Cup fifth round replay, were stranded for eight hours. They were rewarded by their team being defeated by three goals to nil. Following a six-three win over Newport County at Kenilworth Road, the Hatters finished an indifferent season in thirteenth place in Division Two.

Frank appears to have been quite happy and settled at Luton, at least as settled as he ever would be after he left Stoke. Freda moved there and they were living in a sizeable, gable-fronted terraced house belonging to Luton Town Football Club, 24 Kenilworth Road, yards from the ground,. He was also becoming involved with coaching in local schools. Bedfordshire County Council was a forward-looking local authority and was one of the first English counties to set up free coaching to boys over the age of eleven. The sessions were run by the Football Association and the coaches were all professional footballers. Frank spent much of the summer coaching or attending coaching courses. In June, the *Biggleswade Chronicle* reported:

FOOTBALL PROFESSIONAL AT BIGGLESWADE SCHOOL: FRANK SOO SHOWS HOW

> Frank Soo, the Luton right-half, who has also played for Stoke city, Leicester and England, together with Mr A. Tomkins, FA coach, and late of Northampton, Southampton and the Spurs, gave an interesting and much appreciated talk on heading and throwing in at Biggleswade Senior Secondary Modern School on Tuesday afternoon. Frank Soo and Mr Tomkins gave demonstrations of throwing-in, and a number of boys were afterwards picked and practised throwing-in under the watchful eyes of the senior boys and the two experts. After the display, Soo gave a grand display of heading, assisted by Mr Tomkins. The boys were keen learners, and Derek Bygraves put up a fine performance of heading with Soo.

Later that month, Frank and Dally Duncan led an FA-sponsored session coaching "ambitious youngsters from a wide area" at Kempston Barracks. At the end of July he attended a four-day coaching course at Birmingham University. He had clearly made up his mind that his post-playing career would be in coaching in some shape or form.

He was not so settled in Luton, however, that he was not thinking of opportunities in other parts of the world. In the summer of 1947, the Sing Tao Sports Club team, champions of the amateur Hong Kong Football League, came on a short tour of England. It was the first time a Chinese football club had visited the UK, and the tour was seen as a chance to establish closer Sino-British relations after the two countries had fought side-by-side in the Second World War. The tour drew quite a lot of press attention and Sing Tao played against a series of amateur sides, including representative teams from the Isthmian and Athenian Leagues, Dulwich Hamlet, Barnet, Bromley, Ilford, Walthamstow Avenue and Oxford City. The team was featured in the popular magazine *Picture Post* and the tourists were generally made welcome by the press, notwithstanding the odd racist "joke.". They may have been amateurs but the seventeen players who came over from Hong Kong were used to playing before crowds that would not have disgraced a First Division match in England. Local Aldermen and other civic dignitaries were wheeled out to greet the players and they were even taken to see 1066 and All That at the Palace Theatre in London. When the team went back to Hong Kong, their manager, Mr Aw Hoe, revealed that he had invited Frank Soo to consider the possibility of coaching a team in Hong Kong or on the Chinese mainland. The deal failed to happen because it was felt that no team could afford the terms he was asking for. This was reported in the Chinese language newspaper, *Sing Tao Jih Pao* (the *Sing Tao Daily*) - which happened to be owned by Aw Hoe - on 19 September 1947:

> Professional football players in the UK, by regulation, could only maintain their professional status until 34. That is why he [Frank Soo] said should China be interested in hiring him as a coach, he would be more than willing to return to the country for a visit. He would be pleased to accept [the recruitment offer] if [the club concerned] is willing to satisfy his conditions of paying him an annual salary of £500 and covering his travel expenses to Hong Kong and back to the UK in future.

In 1960, another Hong Kong newspaper, *Ta Kung Pao*, revealed a little more detail of why the move never happened: "... he [Frank] indicated that it was not up to him because a transfer fee of at least £5,000 had to be paid to his football club [Luton Town] before he could leave. In those days, nobody would have such courage, or stupidity, to spend such a fortune to hire him."

The Hong Kong Football League would become the first professional league in Asia in 1968. Back in 1947, Frank's demands must have seemed quite incredible. It would not be the last time that Frank Soo attempted to find a role coaching in Asia and suggests that he must have felt that he was competent enough in a Chinese language to take on the role.

The 1947/48 season saw George Martin leave Luton for Newcastle United and Dally Duncan, who had been a great success as a player at Kenilworth Road, took over as manager. Duncan immediately set about strengthening the side and brought in Welsh international full-back, Billy Hughes, which was something of a coup for Luton as several First Division sides were after him. To do so, they had to break the club's transfer record and pay Birmingham £11,000 for him, more than double what Frank Soo had cost them. The season started badly, however, with a one-four defeat at Coventry and Luton continued to have problems scoring goals. Fans were unhappy after Duncan, who stopped playing himself in October 1947 at the age of 39, sold some of their favourite players, including top scorer, Hugh Billington - who had scored twenty-eight goals in the previous season - plus the recently arrived Billy Hughes, after Chelsea came in with an offer of £20,000 for the pair. Duncan brought in some useful players including Bobby Brennan from the Irish club, Belfast Distillery, but it took some time for the side to gel and they finished the season at thirteenth place, exactly the same as they had the previous year.

Nevertheless Frank was among the players that seem to have escaped criticism. His captaincy was picked out by commentators as clever and tactically astute. He was also regarded as being solid defensively. He continued to contribute to the club's activities off the pitch too - as he did at every club he was at - giving talks in village halls and acting as a part-time scout, recommending young players to the club. Whether he had expected to be offered the manager's job is unknown, but he clearly had something of the kind in mind. Whatever happened, there were suddenly rumours of him moving when the season ended. Arthur Rowe, the manager of Chelmsford City, told the Essex newspapers: "We hope to get there [the Third Division] eventually. We continue to put our application to the League, and consider we have quite a strong case. We have already started team building for the next season. Our most important negotiation is with Luton for the services of Frank Soo, One of the best-known ball players in the game." Negotiations, it was reported, were at an advanced stage. While Frank spent the summer coaching the Finnish national team in Helsinki, Freda took the Queen Mary from Southampton to New York.

The Chelmsford manager, Arthur Rowe made it clear how much he wanted Frank in his squad. It was to be a new era for the club, and the ambition was palpable: "I have been looking for a chap who can take the captaincy - a man who can really lead the side. It pleased me no end to think that Frank Soo was interested. Luton demanded a transfer fee. Our directors said: 'Soo is the man we want - go all out for him. Soo is in Finland. If he were here, I have no doubt at all but that I could tell you he was a City player. He will be in Finland until July. I cannot see any snag, but we cannot be sure until we can get his signature."

Rowe pursued Frank's signature relentlessly and he eventually got his man. On 28 May 1948, *Chelmsford Chronicle* announced:

CITY FC PAY A 'SUBSTANTIAL' FEE FOR SOO

Frank Soo, the soccer International, will be coming to Chelmsford City FC.

At a meeting between directors of Luton Town (Soo's present

club) and Chelmsford City, Chelmsford being represented by Alderman F. C. Langton, Mr H. Philip and Mr Arthur Rowe, agreement was reached between the clubs for the transfer of Frank Soo to Chelmsford City. To complete the transfer the player's agreement terms and his signature will have to be obtained, but this will be held up until his return from Finland where he is coaching.

A substantial transfer fee was needed to secure this player, and the directors of the club have taken this burden upon themselves and, in the belief that Soo's value to the team will reward their enterprise.

The acquisition of Frank Soo caused a great deal of excitement in the Essex press. Throughout his time there, the local newspapers, particularly the *Chelmsford Chronicle* and the *Essex Newsman* featured articles and interviews, not only with Frank, but with Freda too, ona regular basis. They were seen as something of a golden couple, and although it would be an absurd exaggeration to describe them as an early "Posh and Becks," the attention they received at this time was remarkable. On 11 June, the press reported that Freda was looking for a house in the area: "Mrs Frank Soo, wife of the famous international ... came to Chelmsford this week to look over the housing accommodation which can be offered to herself and her husband. She was delighted with the house she was shown - the one that has recently been bought on behalf of the club. It is understood that the Luton Town club want the house she is now occupying."

In August, Frank gave an interview to the *Chelmsford Chronicle* in which he talked about his experiences coaching in Finland. It was typical of the kind of press coverage that he would receive while he was in Essex, although this was very much the honeymoon period of his time there:

FRANK SOO'S INTERPRETER WAS HEAD OF JEWISH TERRORISTS!

Blue skies with a few white clouds banked on the horizon, hung over the green of Chelmsford cricket ground while Essex batted leisurely – rather too leisurely – against Somerset at Chelmsford on Wednesday. And while the majority of the spectators, with hats tilted over their eyes, watched or slept, according to their fancy, your columnist sat next to international footballer Frank Soo, now signed by Chelmsford City FC, and chatted – soccer.

Frank has just returned from a trip to Finland where he was coaching. His tales of the country were interesting and punctuated by broad grins. But his face was serious when he told me about his interpreter.

'A nice fellow he was,' said Frank, as he gazed across the cricket field. 'Quite young and apparently friendly. I had known him for thirteen weeks, and was preparing to return to join Chelmsford when he said: "You know, I hate the English."

Someone knocked a ball to the boundary. The voice waited until the spare applause had died, then: 'I was surprised. He had always been friendly enough, so I asked him if he hated me. He didn't. He just hated the English as a whole, and not individually. As I was obviously perplexed, and explained that all the English were much the same as I was, he said: "Do you know who I am? I am the head of the Irgun Zvai Leumi, the Jewish Terrorist Organisation for the whole of Finland!"

Frank laughed at the suggestion that he might have searched his baggage for bombs. There was no need for that of course, he said. This chap was of course a Finnish Jew and responsible for collecting funds for the Terrorist Organisation. He also spread propaganda – but didn't really know why! He had never visited England.

The women:

Frank also spoke about the Finnish women. Thy're tough and very enthusiastic about sport. Javelin and discus throwing is the main excitement and biggest of all – baseball. This is played by women on concrete or cinder tracks and the 'weaker sex' prove mighty tough, flinging themselves full-length after the ball. Other women, up to 40 and over, eagerly dash about in the open doing their 'daily dozen.' And their one, two, up and over, is not done from any sense of duty. They just love it, and pay to do it.

At the end of the mayor's excellent luncheon, Alderman Andrews called on Frank Soo to stand up and show himself to the guests. He did so, and there was very little difference between the colour of his face and a prize beetroot.

Chelmsford City had only been established in 1938, although it was built on the ashes of Chelmsford FC and used the same New Writtle Street stadium. It had become a professional club immediately and joined the Southern League. By the end of the first post-war season in 1946 the club had become league champions. On the strength of this, the club applied unsuccessfully to join the Football League, and as Frank Soo arrived at the club, was still in dispute with the football authorities who had completely rejected the idea of expanding the Football League to four divisions and allowing clubs like Chelmsford entry. Arthur Rowe angrily said that he would continue to press for change and the signing of Frank Soo in a combined role of player, captain and coach, was part of his strategy. Even before he had played a game for the club, expectations were high: "The recent signings of Internationals Frank Soo and Llian O'Neill has brought at touch of football 'class' to the team which they lacked previously. With men of such experience to stiffen the team, and a number of highly promising youngsters coming along, the City should be in a position to please their fans, and furthermore really 'go places.' "

Excitement was high at the prospect of a first glimpse of Soo's artistry in a trial match on 14 August, but Soo, who had been moving house, failed to appear. The local newspaper reported his explanation sympathetically: " 'I had been busy until 3 o'clock this morning,' he said wearily. 'I really did not feel like playing.' " Most commentators appeared to accepted this on face value and didn't pick up on what could easily have been interpreted as a lack of enthusiasm. He was obviously going to play in the first team, after all, so a trial game was unnecessary. It was just a question who would join him in the half-back line. A few days later Frank was more diplomatic, telling the press: "Now that I've got rid of my house-moving problems, I can properly settle down. We should have a reasonably good season."

There is no doubt that Chelmsford City had the idea of increased crowd numbers, and the revenues that would come with it, in mind when they brought Frank Soo to the club. The board of directors and Arthur Rowe made it clear that they had dipped into their own pockets to subsidize his transfer fee. In fact, they never let their supporters forget it, repeating the fact to the press at regular intervals throughout Soo's time at the club. Alderman Langton, vice-chairman of the football club and future mayor of Chelmsford said: "As soon as the season was over we were searching, searching, searching for new players. We 'landed' at Luton and got a contract for Frank Soo. Now I think we are going places – we will continue that progressive policy. I am not boasting or bragging, but I think it is time the public knew that the directors have been dipping and diving their hands in their pockets. Four or five directors have found over £1,300 in order to get the type of player we want. We believe we have found that type of player. No director of the club is in it for what he can get out of it." Whether or not the Chelmsford board made promises to him about the prospect of a future as a player-coach or even manager is not known, but as events panned out, it would seem that it was quite likely that they had. Frank certainly became involved from the beginning in coaching the Chelmsford City Colts, and attended events all over Essex representing the club, including addressing supporters' clubs and going to church services. He appears to have been immensely popular from the beginning, especially with local journalists. Still in August, he was seen to be fitting in very well: "Coming back in the coach from Bedford to Chelmsford on Saturday was a real pleasure. Skipper Frank Soo entered into the spirit of the thing as much as anybody. He sang. So, too, did Jimmy Donnelly, who has a pleasing Irish voice and a seemingly inexhaustible supply of energy."

Frank's arrival at the club made an immediate impact and supporters must have wondered what was in store for the rest of the season. They won the first six matches he played in, including scoring six goals against Kidderminster and Hastings and five against league leaders Merthyr in the Southern League Cup. The run only came to an end with a defeat by local rivals Colchester United at Layer Road. Attendances certainly increased following Frank's arrival at the club, and for some games they more than doubled from the previous season. He quickly won the fans over too. In September 1948, a letter to the *Essex Newsman*, a local supporter, R. E. Gisby wrote:

> Sir, - As a result of Wednesday's City v. United debacle, one or two points have become very clear. Frank Soo is without a doubt the dominating personality in the City team and a player to be respected and listened to by the remainder of the side.
> He proved, along with Pyle, Bidewell and McDermott, that cool-headed football could beat the most unorthodox play which could be put into operation by any opposing team. Colchester's play was to say the least, unorthodox. It was a great pity the remainder of the City team allowed themselves to be shaken out of their usual style of play, which last Saturday was voted unanimously some of the best seen here for many years.

Sports reporters enthusiasm continued too. They were full of admiration for his skills on the field of play and his captaincy: "In Frank Soo the City have a captain who will, I think, mould the players in the side to his liking. The City have lacked the service of a real skipper for some time - in fact, since Alan Sliman. And now I think they have found the man." On 10 September Chelmsford beat Hastings by six goals to nil, the match report gave the credit to "the supremely intelligent work of Soo..." and described his goal - he scored the sixth from a free kick a yard outside the penalty area - as "a beauty." Frank must have enjoyed the game, thrashing a side whose captain, George Skinner, had been his flat-mate in Finland during the summer. Despite injuring his ankle, he continued to play and, following a one-nil away win over Yeovil in November, he was still enjoying a good relationship with both the supporters and the press: "Frank Soo's captaincy had a lot to do with ultimate success in a game which was notable for its rapidly changing fortunes."

Both Frank and Freda seem to have thrown themselves into local life and, at least at first, appeared to be enjoying it. In September, they were both invited to judge a hairdressing competition at the local Press Ball, and Frank, described as a "nifty smiter," played cricket in a City team against Chelmsford Cricket Club at the county ground. As early as December 1948, however, there were signs that Frank was unsettled, although the concerns may have been the result of unfounded newspapers rumours. The *Essex Newsman* reported that Soo might already be leaving Chelmsford:

> Frank Soo Chelmsford City's captain and No. 1 player, whose capture from Luton was a Southern League sensation before the beginning of the present season, told the news Newsman-Herald this morning, 'It's news to me,' when he was questioned about reports that he is likely to return to league football. But he was silent about his own reaction should such a proposal be made. Soo, who was receiving massage to his neck added: 'The first I knew about it [was] when trainer Benny Welham showed me a paper with the report on Sunday morning. I would like to know more about how the news got into the paper. I know nothing about it.'
>
> Mr Arthur Rowe, the city's manager, said: 'The first I heard of anything like that was when I read it in the paper. I cannot confirm or deny the report.'
>
> The news of Soo's possible departure has come as something of a bombshell to City supporters, for Soo – ex-English International wing-half, who has appeared over a dozen times for England – was easily the biggest capture in the City's professional history. His inspired performances have been the brain behind Chelmsford's team work.

The reports, which also appeared in the national press, were taken seriously enough for a denial to be published in the official programme for the next match at New Writtle Street. Another newspaper, the *Chelmsford Chronicle*, responded by suggesting that, in fact, there was a great deal of truth in the story:

> All concerned with the City club's welfare struggled hard and dug deep to build an all-conquering team. Frank Soo was to work a modern miracle and lead the City to fame in another great FA Cup run. It has not happened. Despite Soo's very great efforts and personality the team has no further interest this season either in the FA Cup or the SL Cup. This unfortunately means that a section of the Supporters (who only follow a successful team) will fail to support.
>
> The question will then surely arise of whether or not Frank Soo could be released to go back to League soccer. The cash obtained for him would be most useful in the City coffers and Shalcross would be an admirable substitute. Frank Soo himself has no allegiance to the City. Why should he? There is very

little sentiment in soccer today. It is a commercial proposition. It is not suggested for one moment that Chelmsford want to get rid of Frank, but if he is to go, surely now is a better time from the 'cash' point of view than at the end of the season. Soo is 34. He must start looking for a Coach or Managerial job soon. Personally I should be very sorry to see him go. He is a first-class chap. But if the offer was tempting enough he would undoubtedly take it.

The *Chelmsford Chronicle* sports journalists, J. C. Chaplin and R. A. F. Handley, were close to Frank. It is obvious from all their reports and interviews with him that there was a strong rapport between them and it is likely that he would have confided in them. In fact, in retrospect, it looks as if Frank may have been trying to manipulate events by putting out the suggestion that he could leave, and that League clubs were interested in signing him, he could put pressure on the club. But what did he want in return?

The *Chronicle* continued to cover Frank's appearances on and off the pitch with detailed and sometimes effusive enthusiasm. His goal in January 1949, in a two-two draw against Cheltenham was described thus: "Frank Soo, who had inspired many attacks, scored Chelmsford's opening goal after twenty-five minutes play. The City captain trapped the ball from over thirty yards out. Taking quick but deliberate aim he sent in a powerful shot that hit the upright before re-bounding into the back of the net. Coltman was deceived by the flight of the ball. He was waiting for it to go outside. To him, it was a bolt from the blue."

Likewise, his appearances to play dominoes, darts and crib at supporters' clubs meeting were faithfully chronicled. Even an visit to an old soldiers' club was reported in detail and with the admiration of a fan rather than the words of an objective reporter: "Frank Soo, Chelmsford City left-half and skipper went as a guest to the Royal Engineers Old Comrades re-union dinner on Friday. He was surprised to find himself on the list of speakers. Nevertheless he did well. Through the dinner he made a few notes on his menu and sipped water. When his turn came he rose to his feet without a trace of nervousness. He was given a rousing cheer. He spoke sincerely and convincingly in a clear voice. His theme, a short one, was team spirit. 'I see the team spirit in tonight's meeting,' he said. 'I wish it would spread throughout the world. We would have no more war then.'"

Frank performed well for the rest of the season and retained the admiration of the Chelmsford fans. The club finished as runners-up in the Southern League, one place lower than the previous season. The news that Soo was going to leave City, inevitably described as a "bombshell," hit the front pages of the local press as well as the back ones. Such a furore was as uncommon in non-league football as much then as it would be now. It is worth quoting the newspaper coverage extensively, bearing in mind that some of it, at least, was probably being fed to journalists by both members of the Chelmsford City board and the player himself:

Essex Newsman, 6 May 1949

THE REAL STORY ABOUT FRANK SOO'S DEPARTURE

Directors' offer 'up-to-the-minute' – they think he asked too much for Club finances to justify…. Popular and successful, but there is a limit in £ s. d.

Chelmsford this morning was buzzing with rumours concerning the City Football Club's decision to put their international wing-half captain, Frank Soo, on the transfer list. Yesterday morning this official statement was issued from the New Writtle Street ground.

'With very great regret the directors announce that as Frank Soo has refused the liberal terms offered him for season 1949-50, terms which were considerably increased as from his initial contract of 1948-9, they are left with no alternative but to place this player on the transfer list in accordance with his request.'

I understand however that the Directors of the City club offered Frank Soo terms which they considered reached the limit of their resources. The amount is considerably more than that paid to any First Division professional. And his weekly wage in the summer would have been far more than the pay of the average working man. In the summer it is usual for Frank Soo to take up coaching appointments, and City club's 'retainer' would be plus the amount paid him for outside duties. Moreover, the Directors of the Club are men who have invested considerable sums of money in it. When they sought to obtain Soo from Luton, a substantial transfer fee was involved, and the bulk of this money came from the directors' personal pockets.

They admit Soo has been very popular and a draw on the gate, but not to the extent that would justify his wage demands. Another point, they say, is that he is approaching the veteran stage, and that his football playing days can only last a season or two in Southern League football. They agreed that his coaching and soccer craft have considerably improved the team's display, and they are very loth to lose him.

It must be noted that the Directors are all shrewd business men, who want to see a return on the money laid out, and they are quite agreed, I understand, in the view that the additional cost of any new wage agreement with Soo would not be justified by a foreseeable return in the way of gate money. Another thing which they have in the mind is that the inequality of pay entailed would affect other members of the side. And this would not be for the best advantage of team spirit.

Frank Soo, who says, 'I entirely disagree that there was a considerable increase offered to me,' sums it all up in one sentence: 'The whole point is that the club and I cannot agree as to terms.' "

The Supporters' Club became involved at this stage, but they could do nothing to force the directors to retain Soo's services and, in another shock development, it was announced that Arthur Rowe, had taken the manager's job at Tottenham Hotspur. The vacancy was advertised and, according to some accounts, Frank applied. Rowe pointedly remarked that he would not go until a successor had been appointed. "I want to see everything fixed up before I go," he said.

The Supporters' Club was constitutionally unable to do anything, so supporters began talking to the press in support of not only submitting to Frank's wage demands, but of his being appointed as Rowe's replacement. The following article was accompanied by a photograph of Frank Soo, with the caption "The Man of the Moment":

'WELL WORTH THE MONEY'
BY A SUPPORTER

From the Supporters' point of view, the general opinion is that even though Soo's wage demands may seem excessive, from a playing point of view he is well worth the money.

He has established himself as a firm favourite with all the City fans, and he is the most popular Chelmsford player since the famous V. J. Woodward.

They have further stressed that since his inclusion in the side the standard of football has reached a very high-class. Many Chelmsford men who a year ago went regularly to London or Southend to watch football, are now regular City fans. And many say the class of football seen at New Writtle Street is equal to that of League soccer.

It is understood that the Supporters' Club, who have contributed over £5,000 pounds to the City Club during the post-war season, intend to take the matter up, and will do all in their power to keep Frank Soo as the city player.

The man in the street had the impression that when Arthur Rowe, the manager, left the City Club, the choice of manager would automatically fall on Frank Soo. It was expected that he would act in a similar capacity to that of Ted Fenton when he was with Colchester United, that of player-manager. This news of his impending departure come as a bombshell to all regular City supporters.

On 6 May, just after Arthur Rowe's impending departure had broken, it was announced that Frank had asked to be placed on the transfer list. J. C. Chaplin reported that the reaction to the news was that it was an unmitigated disaster:

> As soon as the announcement was made that Arthur Rowe was leaving the Chelmsford club to return to the 'Spurs, football fans were saying in the streets, in the pubs, in the cinema queues, 'Frank Soo will be manager next season.'
>
> It was thought that Frank might automatically step into Arthur's shoes, so to speak.
>
> I have heard it said many, many times, 'Frank Soo will be a fine successor to Arthur Rowe when he goes.... Frank is the man we want when Arthur goes.'
>
> Now, crashing immediately on top of the news that Mr Rowe, third manager that the club has had in a short but eventful existence, comes the Soo affair. What effect will all this have on the club? What will Soo's departure mean? The City will lose, on the one hand, a manager whose judgment of a player is invariably better than that of his critics. On the other hand, the club will be without the finest skipper it has had since Alan Sliman, also a half-back, lost his life on war service.
>
> Soo's captaincy has been an inspiration to the team. He has thrown himself whole-heartedly into this important job. His generalship will be missed. What, so far as Frank Soo is concerned, is behind it all? It is £ s d. For next season the club have offered what they say in their statement are 'considerably increased terms.'
>
> Frank disagrees with this. That is the crux of the whole matter. And when a player and the club cannot agree on this, the player automatically finds himself on the transfer list. I had a long chat with Soo yesterday. He was, I thought, upset by the turn of events. My impression was that he had intended to stay in Chelmsford for much longer than one season.
>
> 'I like Chelmsford. I am grateful to a splendid lot of supporters and to a fine bunch of players – they have been grand.'

The Chelmsford City directors quickly issued another statement.

STATEMENT BY DIRECTORS

Yesterday morning this official statement was issued from the New Writtle Street ground:

'With very great regret the directors announced that as Frank Soo has refused the liberal terms offered him for season 1949-50, terms which were considerably increased as from his initial contract of 1948-9, they are left with no alternative but to place this player on the transfer list in accordance with his request.'

This decision was made at the weekly Board meeting of the Directors on Tuesday.

"I saw Frank Soo in the dressing room at New Writtle Street yesterday," wrote J. C. Chaplin, who continued, "and asked for his comments on the announcement which have been issued earlier from the club headquarters. I read the details of the announcement to him."

Pondering a moment, Frank said: 'The whole point is that the club and I cannot agree as to terms.'

On two points in the statement Soo emphatically disagreed.

One was this ... 'terms which were considerably increased as over the initial contract of 1948-9.'

He said: 'I entirely disagree that there was a considerable increase offered to me. It was not a considerable increase, in my opinion.'

Soo also disagreed with the phrase ... 'We (the directors) are left with no alternative but to place this player on the transfer list.'

He said: 'The club state that I asked to be put on the transfer list. I would like to say that when terms not suitable between club and player and the club have said that their terms are absolutely final, it is the natural outcome for the player to be placed on the transfer list.'

'Have you any other comment?' I asked.

Soo replied: 'No, except that I shall be very sorry to leave the club. It has all been because of the disagreement on the question of terms. I had hoped to be here the more than a season.'

On Tuesday Mr and Mrs Soo fly to Finland where Frank will continue the coaching upon which he was engaged last year and from where he came to Chelmsford. He will be there during the summer season. Soo may, I understand, take up some important coaching appointments."

Frank spent much of that summer coaching HPS (Helsingen Palloseura), in Finland while the controversy rumbled on in Essex. Just after he and Freda flew out to Helsinki, the *Essex Newsman* revealed that five "well-known" players had applied for Frank's player-coach job. There had also been twelve applications to be manager: "One of the applications has come from as far away as Holland." On 13 May, the *Chronicle* decided to try to explain the situation to its readers. There was talk of supporter protests and this article, although written by one of Frank's admirers, reads as if it had some input from the City board of directors. It began with some surprising news. Soo was staying.

EVERY MAN'S GUIDE THE SOO AFFAIR

The Frank Soo ten-day wonder is taken a stage further with the official announcement that Soo is almost certain to stay with Chelmsford City Football Club after all. No 'pressure' has been brought on the Club by the supporters or anyone else. A compromise figure was offered to Soo.

Here is the official statement from the club: 'The Directors having been informed that Frank Soo agrees to the terms offered by the Club with a minor adjustment to his summer wages, agreements have now been forwarded to Mr Soo in Finland (where he is coaching). With the return of the forms, duly signed, they will be forwarded to the FA for registration for the 1949/50 season.'

But the dust has not yet settled since the eruption into front-page news last week of the impending departure of City Football Club Manager Arthur Rowe to become manager of the famous Spurs.

Strangely enough many are asking "Who is Frank Soo?" Every footballer knows. Others are enquiring politely in much the same way as a famous judge once asked in the courts, "What is a golf-ball?"

Now Frank Soo, captain of Chelmsford City this season, is not only a good footballer. He is also a popular club man and a forceful after-dinner speaker. But the City Directors do not pay for speech-makers. Several of them can manage fairly well on their own. They want deeds on the field and Soo has performed plenty. Immediately before coming here he played for Luton who, it is understood, paid £5,000 by way of transfer fee.

Chelmsford City hoped to get him for nothing. It did not work. ... How much they paid is not available, but the figure of £1,500 was mentioned at the time of the signing a year ago. Directors had to dip into their pockets to find sufficient cash. The problem obviously arose recently of whether it was a financial proposition to keep him for another season at an increased figure, or whether to put him on the transfer list (that is, 'up for sale') and try to recoup some of the money paid out.

Obviously the longer in the tooth, the shorter the price available becomes. That is no reflection on the player. It happens to them all. Frank is 35. His playing days are numbered. No one realises this more that the player himself. That is why he wishes – as all professionals do – to make what he can while the going is good. ... And the going in this case is a bit uphill.

What this means in actual cash and in kind may surprise you.

Frank Soo is considerably better off playing for Chelmsford City than he would be in a First Division Club. The maximum wages are £12 per week in the winter and £10 in the summer. For Soo to have chosen to come here instead of staying in League soccer indicates that Chelmsford were willing to pay a higher sum than that mentioned above.

In addition, he coaches in Finland during our summer months (he flew there on Tuesday), and coaches in this country during the winter when not actually playing.

Chelmsford City also provide him with house – rent-free – worth, say, another £150 a year. The total value of all this must be in the region of £1,250 a year – or £25 pounds a week. Which is not at all bad for a footballer no longer in his prime.

The City Directors must have decided that they have a chance of a reasonable financial return. They are all astute business men. This trading in football flesh is very much a strict matter of cash. When the flesh grows week – then the cash grows weak with it.

The directors may have wanted it to be known that the deal with Frank was not the result of any pressure being put on them, but the tone of the article suggests that they were not entirely happy with the player's demands for more money. In early June, the *Chronicle* suggested another way the two sides might reach a financial compromise:

CITY LIKELY TO 'SIGN' MRS FRANK SOO

Mrs. Soo – wife of Frank – is likely to be the latest signing' on the Chelmsford City FC books. On Tuesday the Club Directors will meet to decide whether Frank Soo or Len Goulden (English International and Chelsea left-half, and former Chelmsford player) is to be the City's new player-manager. If Frank is chosen, then Mrs Soo will come also – as paid Secretary to Frank.

This is the form. Seven applicants are still officially listed for consideration for Arthur Rowe's job. But only Soo and Goulden are among the probables. One of these two will be chosen. If it is Frank, then he will have to cancel his Finland contract, where he is coaching, and return right away – at a financial loss. This will be made up by taking on Mrs Soo as a paid secretary to Frank. Frank's new contract stipulates £15 a week in the winter and £12 a week in the summer. The club would be asked to pay his wife £150 a year for Secretarial duties. It is likely they will accept.

Whether the offer was actually made or not - the confusion was not helped by the announcement by Arthur Rowe that Frank had not even applied for the manager's job - is not clear. The newspapers confidently predicted that there was a shortlist of five, but one of only two men would become the new Chelmsford City manager, Len Goulden from Chelsea or Frank Soo. The club said that they had received Frank's completed player registration forms back from Finland. Then there was a further surprise. The story made the front page of the *Chronicle*:

JACK TRESADERN LIKELY FOR CITY MANAGER'S JOB

All was ready at a late hour last night for the signing of Mr Jack Tresadern, formerly Manager of West Ham, to succeed Mr Arthur Rowe as a manager of the Chelmsford City Football Club. Mr Tresadern has been team manager of Northampton, Crystal Palace, Tottenham Hotspur, and Plymouth, whom he joined in 1938. His playing career was spent with West Ham, and in 1923 he represented England against Scotland as a half-back.

The choice came as a surprise. On Tuesday the City Directors stated that they had chosen Len Goulden, of Chelsea. But Chelsea decided they wanted to keep Goulden, and offered him cash to stay on. So the Chelmsford City Directors held another meeting yesterday, when they unanimously decided that Jack Tresadern, who had previously applied to the job, was the man they wanted.

It is understood that Frank Soo's application for the managership failed because – although an excellent footballer and club man – he lacked managerial experience.

If Frank had ever been led to believe that he had a future as the manager of Chelmsford City, this must have come as a blow to him. No one was able to fault his commitment to his club. He had played and captained the side for two seasons, participated in all kinds of events on behalf of the club, coached and scouted. He was in a bind that seems to still affect young, aspiring black managers in Britain to this day. He was not given the job because of lack of experience, but he would never gain that experience until he was appointed to a managerial post. The man who was chosen as manager, Jack Tresadern, did have considerable experience, having been a manager since his playing career had been ended by a broken leg in 1926. He had managed Crystal Palace, Tottenham Hotspur and Plymouth Argyle, but his first management job had been when he went straight from player to manager at Northampton Town, with no experience whatsoever. No one seemed to be prepared to give Frank Soo a similar chance, despite acknowledging his qualities as a player and coach.

Meanwhile, Frank was enjoying himself in Scandinavia. As well as coaching in Finland, he managed to find time to play in two friendlies for Köping FF. According to *Dagens Nyheter*, he was visiting his "old friend," Kalle Gustafsson who had longstanding connections with Leicester City and he appears to have played as a guest in the friendlies while he was there. His appearance caused some consternation as to whether he was setting some kind of precedent that allowed professional footballers to play in amateur sides, but he was a success on the pitch and, in one of the games, Köping beat the Danish side, Kjøbenhavns Boldklub by three goals to nil.

Frank had a longstanding friendship with Kalle Gustafsson and his son Tage. Important figures in Swedish - and Scandinavian - football, it is likely that many of Frank's contacts in the game there and in Finland, came through them. His future clubs as manager included Eskilstuna, Örebro, Djurgårdens and Köping, all of which had connection with Swedish football's elder statesman, Kalle Gustafsson.

The Swedish daily, *Aftonbladet*, reported on his other game for Köping provides more detail:

> Danish division two club Hellerup, from Copenhagen, started their Swedish football tour, which the Köping Sports Club is hosting, this past Sunday. The first match was played in Köping, who were being impolite hosts and beat the Danes by 4-2. This result is, however, very flattering for the rising division four team, who in large part will have to ascribe the victorious honour to the sensational addition, provided for a day, by the English-Chinese professional player Frank Soo. As it happens, Soo, who for 19 seasons has played in the half back position behind Stanley Matthews in Stoke, is coaching the Finnish national team this summer, but was temporarily visiting Köping, where he was staying with Köpings' Gustafsson. When Soo

was asked whether he might not be interested in playing in the international match between KIS [Köping Sports Club] and Hellerup, he immediately made himself available at no charge, and the Swedish Football Federation also gave its permission. He displayed excellent half back play and contributed greatly to amassing a crowd of nearly 2,000 people who watched the enjoyable match.

Frank was due back in August 1949 for pre-season, but it seems that things were still not as they should be between player and club. A full-strength squad was due to play in a trial match at the New Writtle Street Stadium on 13 August, but Frank was still in Finland. He sent a cablegram to Jack Tresadern: "Regret unable to make 13th. Letter following. Regards, Soo."

He was back for the start of the season proper, however, and Tresadern moved him to inside-left. Things did not go well for the City side, but the local press, at least, were prepared to give the new manager a chance: "The structure is there, but the gaps need to be filled quickly, or public support will soon drop." Once again, it was Frank Soo who was winning the plaudits, particularly for his "fine generalship," but he must have been contemplating his future, already having considered working in China and Scandinavia recently. This time, external events took a hand. On 24 October 1949, Freda's beloved father, Thomas Lunt, died suddenly following a heart attack, at the age of only fifty-eight. Freda left for North Staffordshire, apparently permanently, and a few weeks later on 17 November, Frank was again placed on the transfer list at his own request, this time because he wanted to move to a club nearer to his wife.

It was obvious that there was more to it than that. The following day, the *Chelmsford Chronicle* devoted most of its front page to the discord that existed between Frank and his manager. Underneath photographs of the two, the sports editor finally made public a dispute that had clearly been rumbling on for months:

> Chelmsford City Football Club Directors had a stormy meeting on Tuesday, at the end of which they reluctantly decided to place club captain Frank Soo on the transfer list. Soo had previously asked the Board to release him from his contract for 'domestic circumstances and responsibilities.'
> This they were not prepared to do, but hope by placing him on the transfer list to recover the cash they paid out for his services two seasons ago. This is understood to exceed £2,000.
>
> There are several reasons – apart from the official one – for Soo's sudden decision. They are as follow:
> • Misunderstanding, for some time between City Manager Jack

Tresadern v. Frank Soo, has erupted into the open dispute;

• Frank describes himself as having been 'definitely unhappy' with Chelmsford City over a period of several months;

• Mrs Soo is also unhappy living in Chelmsford and is returning to Stoke-on-Trent to be near her mother who was recently bereaved.

• Soo adds: 'Tresadern's manager; I am Captain. Our ideas don't coincide. One of us must go – so it better be me.'

The Chairman of the Supporters' Club expressed his unhappiness and called an emergency meeting and on page seven of the same issue, another article appeared, alongside a photograph of Freda, who declared "I am tired of the whole business. I shall be glad to get back to Stoke."

Once again, local journalists attempted to explain what was going on to supporters who must have been extremely puzzled by the whole affair, not least because the timing - at a crucial stage of the club's FA Cup campaign - was dreadful. This time things were becoming nasty, and the restrained politeness of the previous disagreements was left behind:

It is evident that the breach between management and club captain is a wide one. It cannot be healed. Neither can it be covered by describing it as 'domestic circumstances and responsibilities,' although Mrs Soo undoubtedly has urgent personal reasons for wishing to return to Stoke-on-Trent. 'And,' Frank says, 'how can I go on living alone down here with my wife up there?'

Here is the real story. Fans must judge for themselves.

Three weeks ago Mrs Soo's father died very suddenly. That, undoubtedly so far as Frank and his wife were concerned, influenced their decision to get out of Chelmsford and return to Stoke as quickly as possible. Both have been unhappy here for some considerable time. There are unlikely to be tears shed by either side at the parting.

One of the City FC Directors told me on Wednesday: 'I could give you many examples to show that Soo has been "difficult" with us. He did not "hit it off" with the previous manager, Arthur Rowe. Now it is the same with Jack Tresadern. Is the manager always wrong?

He alleged that there were occasions when Soo was 'arrogant,' even 'dictatorial.' Directors, he complained, were made 'to eat humble pie' in order to keep Soo from walking out. Needless to say, Soo treats all such allegations as ridiculous.

Jack Tresadern, I was told, was sore because Frank nipped off to Stoke without first seeking the club Manager's permission. That was three weeks ago, when Frank's father-in-law suddenly died.

'But,' explains Frank, 'it was no deliberate insult. I was in a very great hurry, and had already obtained permission from two of the Club Directors.'

It is doubtful whether that explanation satisfies Tresadern. For the last two weeks he has not included Soo in his Southern League team selection. Apparently only the intervention of Directors saved Soo from playing for the Reserves.

'Childish,' comments Frank. 'In any case, I should enjoy playing for the Reserve side. I have always tried to do my best to the Club in anyway I can.'

It has also been brought up against Soo that he failed to attend a tactical talk given by Tresadern just before the Barnet game last week. All the others went. Frank, however had a snooze in the coach. 'I hadn't been told it was on,' he said.

Soo is 35. He knows that League clubs are 'cagey' about signing a footballer of that age.

'I am good for another five years,' he said on Wednesday. 'But they decide on age - not ability.'

So the Directors chances of recovering their £2,000 'plus' look a bit thin. Soo, still under contract, must continue to play if chosen to do so. He will be absent this week owing to injury.

Soo's final crack: 'I suggested release from my contract as being the best thing for the club and myself. By doing so they would save the Club £15 a week and themselves the embarrassment of having a dictatorial and arrogant player.'

It was obviously not a state of affairs from which either side could recover. There was no love lost between Tresadern and Frank Soo and the club's directors were anxious to rid themselves of him, as long as they could get their money back. Frank's attitude seems uncharacteristically abrasive. No doubt he was still angry about the way he had been treated over the manager's job. It was hard for him not to resent Tresadern, but the new manager does not appear to have behaved with much sensitivity towards his player. It seems particularly insensitive to have brought matters to a head publicly so soon after Freda's bereavement. The suddenness of her father's death - and she was very close to him - appears to have had a very serious effect on her, one which would have repercussions not so long afterwards that would change things forever.

The Supporters' Club went so far as to suggest that Tresadern should be removed and Soo appointed player-manager. They were desperate to keep him. Chelmsford may not have been a one-man team, but, despite his age, Frank's skills and artistry were still a cut above what fans were used to at New Writtle Street, and they knew it. It was too late. The directors wanted £1,000 for their player and Kidderminster Harriers offered to pay it, but Frank turned the offer down, slightly contradicting his claim that he wanted to move back to the midlands. "I may take up coaching work in schools," he told reporters. The whole situation descended into an embarrassing squabble as accusations flew back and forth between the Supporters' Club, the press, the City directors and even the players, who took umbrage at a remark, attributed to Frank, that they lacked team spirit. The City goalkeeper, Joe Crozier, wrote to the club's Directors on behalf of the players:

> The Chairman, the Board of Directors.
> Sir, – The players of your Club have nominated me to send this letter to you in which they hope to convey to you their feelings with regard to the recent statements which have appeared in the Press.
> The players feel somewhat slighted and very indignant that the Club Captain should declare openly that there is no team spirit. They wish to deny any such allegations.
> There is no dissension among the players, either in the dressing-room or on the field of play, and we all feel sure that past and future relations will prove to the directors and management that every player is 100 per cent. club men.
> Finally, we would like you to know that the players have every confidence in the directors and the management, and we feel sure that the happy family spirit will be prevalent throughout our association with the Club, which we all hope will be a very lengthy one.
>
> J. CROZIER
> pp. The Players

The accusation never appeared in the press, in fact, but was made privately by Soo in a meeting with the board. Following the publication of this letter, it must have seemed to Frank that there was no going back.

The supporters of Chelmsford City Football Club had other ideas however. Frank was forced to play in the Reserves and many fans went to watch them instead of the first team. On occasions there were bigger crowds at Reserves matches who began to do much better, even looking like contenders for the Eastern Counties League title. "City Man," reporting in the Chronicle quoted comments from the spectators: "If only he had been playing against Ipswich" and "He is badly wanted in the first-team." The newspaperman agreed and wondered how long it would be until

Frank forced himself back into the Southern League, but Tresadern was unforgiving and Frank remained in the Reserves into the new decade.

The supporters began a letter writing campaign. In January 1950, "J. F. F." of Ingatestone wrote:

> Sir, - The majority of Chelmsford City supporters, after watching Saturday's game with Gravesend, will not be looking forward to the approaching Cup-tie with Colchester with any great confidence. Individually, with perhaps one or two exceptions, one cannot find much fault with the City players, but they are definitely not playing together as a team. What they lack is obviously a real captain, one who can lead them, hold them together, one who can call for that little extra and get it. One with all the finer points of football at his finger-tips. Now the club have such a man on their books, but where is he?
>
> Playing for the Reserves or, as last Saturday, not playing at all – Frank Soo.
>
> What the supporters want to know is why, when we all know that he is fit, is he not leading the First team. If Colchester had him would they play him in their reserves?

Other letters came in from anonymous fans:

> Sir – Could you tell the public why our old friend and sportsman, Frank Soo, is still out of the 'City' team. My friends and I still think that Frank is one of the best half-backs in the Southern League. ...
> ONE OF THE MANY CITY SUPPORTERS
> Chelmsford
> (Name and address supplied)

> Sir, - What has come over the Chelmsford City football team? On the last two occasions on which I saw them play I was appalled at the seeming lack of cohension, team spirit, and will to win. What is the explanation after the failure to build up a team worthy of the County Town, notwithstanding the generous expenditure of money and the importation of big names?
>
> Is it correct to assume that better men are standing on the touch-line as so many supporters maintain...?
> A LOYAL SUPPORTER
> P.S. If you publish this will you please withhold my name.

At first team games, supporters began chanting "We want Soo." The directors, perhaps conscious they were still paying him £15 a week, relented following a "lively" two-hour meeting, and by mid-January he was back in the first team. No offers had come in from other clubs. His return was greeted with a rather over-enthusiastic reponse by John Parker of the *Essex Newsman*:

> Although the Directors and Management have declined to comment on the return of Frank Soo to the Chelmsford City team as captain for tomorrow's game, it is obvious that this revolution in the team has been caused by popular demand. The fans want the return of the man who has impressed himself so much on the football world in this area as a natural leader on the field.
>
> However popular or unpopular Soo may be with the Management and players at the Club (and there are many disturbing rumours about friction) it is a matter of intense psychological interest that once on the field of play Soo has the priceless gift of leadership so rare that when appears it is greeted with cries of admiration.
>
> Football crowds are made up of men and women of all classes, all kinds of mentality. In fact, they are cross-sections of the people. And with the people leadership is the one thing that counts. They respond to it with instant recognition. ...
>
> What is Frank Soo like to meet, to talk to?
>
> Most people here know him as the shortish, dark man who moves with machine-like efficiency about the field, rarely flustered, calling quick, sharp orders to his team, distributing telling passes to his forwards, covering gaps in the defence, and, above all, holding his team together and welding them into one unit.
>
> Personally he is very like that – unemotional, imperturbable, quick thinking, slow of speech, and of impressive personality.
>
> He shakes hands firmly, no nonsense, and immediately gets down to the business in hand. He is friendly, but unyielding. It is easy to see that he could make enemies, and could be an unequally implacable foe himself.
>
> Above all he shows his determination to succeed in whatever he does.
>
> This, in my opinion, is the secret of his success with the crowds and his inspiring effect on the rest of the team.
>
> In that process he may have become unpopular.
>
> There are rumours about his aloofness, how he will speak to very few of the other players.
>
> People have seen him on the New Writtle Street ground at training, not with the others, the jog-trotting round by himself.

He may have made himself disliked by such methods as this.

Yes almost everywhere, leadership appears. So does unpopularity.

Take the case of Monty, the greatest soldier of our time. Many people criticise his methods. But no one in the Forces who served under him would deny him that inspiring quality of leadership.

Take the case of Churchill, the greatest statesman of our time. Without doubt he has made many enemies as friends. Some people say that leadership is born in a man, others say it can be instilled.

Lord Wavell had to wait many years as a Colonel before he became a Major General...

And you cannot have truly efficient team work unless it conforms to the ideas, inspiration, and example of one man.

In Chelmsford City FC that man is Frank Soo.

The fans have recognised this, as men always recognise a leader of men. And they have called Soo back.

Letters have been flooding into Chelmsford City football ground and into this newspaper office, all saying one thing: 'bring back Frank Soo.'

And whatever the internal differences off the Club, the management on Tuesday decided to bow to the popular demand. The one man the fans think can pull the City together has returned to the first-team after weeks on the touch-line. FRANK SOO IS BACK. FOR MANY FANS SAY HE IS INDISPENSABLE.

His return was hugely successful. "It was worth 1s 3d of anyone's money merely to see Frank's twinkling feet," the *Chronicle* reporter said. Frank Soo had a point to prove and he was playing some of the best football of his time at Chelmsford. "Class was written on his every move," according to one writer.

In March 1950, he came down with shingles which meant that he could not play for a few weeks. He was sorely missed. Once again, he had made himself indispensable and by the end of the season, he was somewhat surprisingly put on City's list of retained players. Inevitably, Frank would have the last word and on 12 May he told the *Chelmsford Chronicle* that he was leaving. "I have considered this matter very carefully over a long time. I have decided to pack up active football and shall go over to full-time coaching." He accepted the post of full-time coach at Isthmian League club, St Albans, on 30 May. "He and Mrs Soo will be leaving Chelmsford for St Albans very soon," the *Essex Newsman* told its readers and by mid-July they had moved into their new home on the outskirts of the Hertfordshire town.

"I'll be very busy coaching," Frank said in his final interview. "Not only the St Albans players, but the local schoolboys for a long way around. ... It's just what I like. ... I shall be very happy. They're nice people, and already we seem to have made friends. ... All the same, I shall never forget Chelmsford, particularly the City Supporters, who, I felt, were always friends of mine...."

5

'SLAVDRIVARE'
St Albans, Padova, Scandinavia, Scunthorpe, 1950 - 1961

The Essex newspapers kept the Frank Soo story going over the summer break. Many supporters felt that, as he had been put on Chelmsford City's list of retained players, there was still a chance that he would be back, but as the J. C. Chaplin explained in the *Essex Newsman* on 2 June 1950, Frank was very excited about the move: "So Frank Soo is leaving Chelmsford in about a fortnight. I am sorry - and so are many more. The City captain for the past two seasons has got a job which, to use his own words, he will revel in. At St Albans he will be full-time coach to the Isthmian League club." Frank left the interview to play bowls for the Chelmsford Division Police, something that he had been doing regularly for a while. Essex would miss him.

Frank was particularly excited that his new job would involve coaching young people in schools from all over the district. "I shall be very happy there," he said. "I may apply for my reinstatement as an amateur, but I don't intend to play anything like regularly. I may play once or twice. But in my own interests I shall carry on full-time training. I don't intend to get stale." It's hard to imagine that Frank had seriously given very much thought to not playing. Like his former teammate at Stoke City, Stanley Matthews, he believed that he could go on for as long as he was able to stay fit. He couldn't give it up and would have played on for years longer, had anybody wanted him to.

He wanted to make an impact in his first post as a club coach and two St Alban's players, inside forward Ken Facey, and half-back John Morrison had been moved out to Leyton FC before the end of June. There would be other departures before the season even began. In early July, advertisements appeared in the *Luton News*:

ST ALBANS CITY FOOTBALL CLUB
(Coach: Frank Soo)
Invite applications from Senior and Junior players.
Full training and social facilities

Still the Chelmsford City fans thought their idol might return. In September and October the local press tried to quash rumours that Frank Soo was coming back to Essex. Even the club's secretary, F. J. Turner, wrote in the match programme that "that stalwart Frank Soo" would be missed in the the the forthcoming season as if to make the point that Clarets' fans had seen the last of him. Still the rumours continued. On 1 December 1950 the *Essex Newsman* was still trying to put the message across: "Kill that rumour that Frank Soo has left St Albans City. He hasn't. He has never been happier."

If Frank had never been happier, then the events of the first few months of 1951 are difficult to understand. By April, he was coaching a side in the Italian Serie A and was separated from his wife. Freda had gone back to live with her mother in North Staffordshire and taken up hairdressing again in Newcastle-under-Lyme. The marriage was over.

No one knows what happened between Frank and Freda Soo. There are not many people who remember them now, but those who do, talk about a golden couple, a perfect couple. Indeed, some of the problems that Frank had with his clubs when he was a player were centred upon his wish to have his wife near to him, and for her to be happy. The all-too-obvious explanation - that one of them had found someone else - does not seem to be borne out by later events. Frank has been described to me, by several members of his family, as "a ladies' man," but when pushed to elaborate that well-worn phrase, most people seem to mean simply that women loved him. He was charming, certainly, but there is no evidence that he was unfaithful to Freda or involved with anyone else. The early 1950s was a time when people were much more reticent about discussing marriage breakdown, but in the period just after the Second World War there was also a massive increase in the number of divorces in Britain and it was much more common than it had been before the war. It seems unlikely that no one among their family and friends would be able to remember what had happened if there had been a scandal at that time. Besides, as someone who knew both Frank and Freda, and had some thoughts on what might have happened, told me, "It was a long time ago and they are both dead. It really doesn't matter now." Frank never remarried and from this time onwards, he appears to have been quite alone.

Why and how did Frank Soo team up with Padova? In late February 1951 Frank was still coaching schoolboys in Biggleswade and still the manager of St Albans City FC, but his name was also beginning to appear in the Italian press, particularly in the *Corriere dello Sport*. In mid-April it was announced that Frank Soo was the new head coach of Padova (Padua in its English form) following the dismissal of Giovanni Ferrari. He appears to have still been officially manager of St Albans until the end of the season, when the English club finished ninth in the Isthmian League. It was a disappointing season and it's likely that the directors of St Albans were not too unhappy to see Frank move on, but nothing really explains the suddenness of his departure.

Frank Soo was by no means the first British footballer in Serie A. William Garbutt, who coached Genoa from 1911 to 1929, and Bob Spotishwood, who went from playing for a Yorkshire colliery side, Elsecar Main, to managing Inter Milan in 1922 preceded him. More recently, William Chalmers Scott had moved from Ebbw Vale to coach Juventus in 1948 and John Astley had been at Inter in 1948/49. *Il Padova* itself had employed Englishman Herbert Burgess, a former player for both Manchester United and Manchester City, in the 1920s. So Frank's arrival in Italy was nothing new.

Italy had a long tradition of employing foreign managers and there were a number of former players from Austria and Hungary who had long and successful coaching careers in Italy, including Gyula Lelovich and Ernesto Erbstein. Interestingly, the description of Erbstein's management style at *Il Grande Torino* chimes strongly with that of Frank Soo: "He forced his players to work for hours with repetitive exercises, which they hated, but which led to excellent results." (John Foot, *Calcio*.) It might have been Frank's reputation for toughness that attracted Padova and it was perhaps also felt that this was a type of coaching which was best imported. There were also more and more Scandinavians becoming involved in Italian football, either as players or coaches. Gunnar Gren, Gunnar Nordahl, Nils Liedholm (the great Gre-No-Li trio of Milan) and Lennart Skoglund, are just a few examples of Swedish players who were in Italy in 1950 and it's likely that Frank would have known them, and many other players, through his connections in the Swedish game. George Raynor had brought the amateur Swedish national team to London for the 1948 Olympic Games and returned to Sweden with the gold medal. English coaches were highly regarded in Europe and Frank's reputation as a teammate of Stanley Matthews and an England international footballer - his nine caps did not look "unofficial" to the rest of the world - would have helped his case.

The football club in Padova was originally founded in 1910, but had gone through several incarnations, including during the 1930s when it was known as the Associazione Fascista Calcio Padova. Having dropped the fascist allegiance, the club was now known as the Associazione Calcio Padova and had been promoted to Serie A at the end of the 1947/48. Frank arrived after a poor start to the season under Giovanni Ferrari. Universally referred to as "mister Soo" in Italy, he took charge on 12 April 1951. Although his Chinese ethnicity was mentioned occasionally in the Italian press, for the most part he was referred to as "*il inglese.*"

His new side had some notable players including Enrique Martegani, an Argentinian attacking midfielder, and Celestino Celio, but most of Padova's players would have indifferent careers in clubs that hovered between the bottom of Serie A and the lower divisions. Frank's first duty was to watch Padova play a friendly against the lower league side Schio, a game that the *Corriere dello Sport* described as a "lacklustre test." His comment that "there was much work to do," was tactful but honest. He needed time, it was a question of whether the club would give it to him.

His first game as coach would be against Como, just a few days after a nil-nil draw at home against Atalanta had left both the club and its supporters angry and disappointed. The press reported accusations of laziness against the players and ineptitude against the President, Valentino Cesarin. Soo started as he meant to go on. The team trained hard, as he "tirelessly" put them through a regime of "prolonged athletic and exercise sessions." If the club had recognized it needed its players to shape up, they had brought in the right man to do it. Despite two key players, Sforzin and Quadri, being out with injuries, Padova beat Como by three goals to one. Results went badly after that, however, and the new tough training system could only have been sustained if it meant success on the pitch. After a goalless draw against Triestina, Padova lost their next four matches against Lucchese, Novara, Genoa and Juventus. Although they won their last game of the summer against Napoli, two-nil at home, they finished the season in eighteenth place with twenty-nine points. "Although we have the utmost respect for the British style," wrote a *Corriere* journalist, "with regard to a Padua remodeled and rejuvenated, it is a little too much for a race that does not have all that characteristic combativeness."

In Italy Frank was to find the clichés that dogged his career were at least being used to refer to more than one kind of national stereotype. *La Stampa* thought "mister Soo... combined oriental resignation with British fair play" and the flowery prose writing of the Italian press even managed to refer to him as a "helmsman," presumably a reference to Chairman Mao, mainly because he appears to have taken a river boat trip with one of his players. In June 1951, the situation at Padova was being described as precarious, the defeat to Juventus only being acceptable because of who their opponents were. They were hovering in the relegation zone and what was even more worrying was that they looked in worse shape than their nearest rivals, both technically and in terms of morale. Soo kept his players in what was described as a "kind of cloistered life" in a hotel in Abano, about twelve kilometres from Padua and they were kept there until just before the final match of the season on 17 June. They beat Napoli 2-0, perhaps because the players were afraid of what Soo would do to them if they lost.

The tough training regime continued over the summer. The *Corriere dello Sport* started referring to the coach as "Yes, sir, mister Soo." Quadri was transferred to Como and Soo tried to bring in a Norwegian, Knut Andersen, but the transfer was delayed until he finally received clerance from the Scandinavian Federation in December. There were rumours that Padova were about to sign the former Danish international, Johannes Pløger from Torino as well, but he eventually went to Udinese.

For the opening game of the new campaign against Pro Patria, Frank brought in three "rookies," Sessa, Camporese and Sperotto. Young Bruno Camporese, who had come through Padova's youth setup, came in at the problematic inside left position. Despite looking promising, especially defensively, the new look *biancorossi* side drew with Pro Patria, both teams scoring two goals. Padova lost their next two matches, at home to Como and away to Napoli. From being their fellow relegation candidates in the previous season, Napoli now regarded Padova as an easy target and Soo received some mild criticism for what was perceived as the pretentious decision to fly his team to Naples rather than travel by coach or train. The two-nil victory was very satisfying for Napoli who had until recently regarded Padova as a bogey side. Having managed a win against Bologna, Soo's side won again when they played Lucchese, but their short run of good form - the match at Lucca was "endured rather than enjoyed" according to the *Corriere dello Sport* - confidence was still low when they went to meet a Torino side that featured the likes of Amalfi, Forio and Carapellese in its attack. Fuchs had been sent off against Lucchese and the team was unsettled by transfer rumours (Sforzin and Giusti were thought to be going to Venezia). A heavy defeat was predicted and it came with four Torino goals to only one by their visitors. Nevertheless, what followed was a mixed run of two draws, against Atalanta and Legnano and a victory over Lazio on 4 November 1951. A defeat by Fiorentina was followed by a good win over in form side Bologna, with two goals from Martegani, but according to the match report in the *Corriere dello Sport*, "the success of the *biancorossi* was welcomed by their tribe of supporters jubilantly [but] has not softened the mouths of [their] critics."

A week later they were to play the Champions, AC Milan. Soo worked hard to finally get Andersen's transfer deal done and he went straight into the first team. His players were only undertaking light training in preparation for this match which sold out, with tickets being purchased on the black market. Soo reconfigured his team. Andersen and Sperotto would play the roles of *mezz'ala*, outside midfielders, with Martegani on the right wing and Prunecchi on the left. It was an attacking line up and with Fuchs returning from suspension at left back, Soo had more of the kind of team he wanted. It worked. Despite facing the great Swedish Gre-No-Li attack and Lorenzo Buffon's goalkeeping, Padova beat Milan by five goals to two.

The second half of the season did not go well. Despite a few wins, mainly against the division's weaker sides like Pro Patria, Padova went on a run of poor form, losing to Internazionale (4-0), SPAL (2-4), Juventus (3-0), Como (3-2), Napoli (0-1), Bologna (2-1) and Lucchese (0-1). By March, things were looking grim. They were about to face Torino on 16 March, but three days before, it was suddenly announced that Soo had gone. *La*

Stampa reported that the *biancorossi* were "currently in a leadership crisis. After the expulsion [*d'allontanamento*] of Mr. Soo, Padova, entrusted to the care of the coach ... [Gastone] Prendato [who had played for Padova during the 1930s]... Given the gravity of the situation, the leaders are determined to engage a new coach."

What *La Stampa* did not know, or did not share with its readers anyway, were the circumstances of Frank's departure from the club. The shocking news had come from his wife's family in Staffordshire that Freda had died on 10 March 1952. He flew back to England and stayed with his mother-in-law in her house in Mill Lane, Wetley Rocks. He did not get back to England in time for the inquest into Freda's death. Evidence was given in court that "Mr Soo was travelling in Italy at the present time."

Freda had died as a result of taking an overdose of barbiturates. Her sister, Gwendolyn, gave evidence that she had been upset since she and Frank had separated twenty months before. She had had a nervous breakdown, been very depressed and was unable to sleep. She had moved to Newcastle-under-Lyme and had been working as a hairdresser. Elizabeth Brownsword gave evidence saying that "when she saw Mrs Soo in her hairdressing shop last Thursday she was crying and very depressed. She seemed almost to be in utter despair. The shop was closed and Mrs Soo put to bed. According to reports of the inquest, she was found dead in bed the following morning, although her death certificate states her place of death was the City General Hospital in Stoke-on-Trent. The Coroner recorded death by barbiturate poisoning, but not one of suicide. He decided that Freda had probably taken too many of the barbiturates in an attempt to get some sleep, adding "I do not think that I am justified in the circumstances in saying that she did it with the intention of ending her life.

Freda was only thirty-six years old when she died and still married to Frank Soo. She was buried in the quiet moorland churchyard of St John the Baptist, Wetley Rocks, beside her father. When her husband died forty years later, he would not be buried beside her.

Frank's official contract at Padova lasted until 30 June 1952, but he didn't go back to Italy. Freda had died intestate but probate gave everything she had, £591 10s 6d, to him, as her lawful husband, in April that year. The probate documents give his address as 43 Mill Road, Wetley Rocks, which was Freda's mother's home and he appears to have still been on good terms with Freda's family. By May that year though, he had moved on again. This time he signed a one-year contract to coach the Swedish club, Eskilstuna. He was engaged to do another job before he moved to Sweden however. In June it was announced that Frank had also been appointed the head coach of the Norwegian Olympic team for the Helsinki games in July 1952. The *Dagens Nyheter*, describing him as "Eskilstuna's distinguished football manager," reported that Soo's "Swedish employers had responded to Norwegian wishes" but were certain to reclaim their coach after "the Norwegian excursion." The brief item did not consider how much he would be able to contribute in such a short time. Frank would only be able to work with the Norwegian side just before and during the tournament, presumably having been brought in because of his reputation for tough training regimes. Perhaps Norway were also hoping to replicate the success that their Swedish neighbours had in the 1948 Olympics in London, when they hired the Englishman George Raynor to coach their football team and won the gold medal. Given the short time he had, Soo could hardly be blamed for Norway's spectacularly poor tournament. They lost (4-1) in the first round to a strong Swedish side who would go on to take the bronze medal after losing 6-0 to the eventual gold medal winners, Hungary - a team that included Zoltán Czibor and Ferenc Puskás.

Eskilstuna City, known as IK City in this era, had begun in 1907 in a city in south eastern Sweden that was best known for its steel manufacturing industry. The football club has never been especially successful. Its highest achievement to this day has been twelfth place in the Allsvenskan (the top division in Sweden) in 1925/26. So it created some excitement when the start of the 1952/53 season went so well. "CHINESE TRANSFORMS CITY TO A GREAT TEAM WITH A NEW STYLE OF PLAY" was the headline in *Expressen* on 17 September. The article below the headline was illustrated by a photograph of Soo with his players. He was dressed in a smart suit and looked noticeably older than he had when he was at Chelmsford. City had just defeated another steel town's team, Sandvikens IF by three goals to nil. The *Expressen* reporter had no doubt that it was the new manager who had transformed Eskilstuna into a "new and better" side. He had quickly managed a "metamorphosis" in the defence. He wanted a different style of play, "long, sweeping passes," adding that "He never tires of preaching this gospel to his adepts." The writer paid fulsome tribute to Frank's work ethic. "He has a tremendous desire to work and work." Not only was he in charge of the first team, but also the youth team, as well as coaching at local elementary and grammar schools. On top of all this Frank was commuting to Eskilstuna from Köping, over forty kilometres away. It is obvious to conclude that Frank was throwing himself into work in order to try to recover from the tragedy of his wife's death, but it is nevertheless probably true. He always had a strong commitment to his work - it's unlikely, given his passion for the game, that he even thought of it as work - but now he was filling up his time so completely he must have little time to think of anything else at all.

Soon after he returned from the Helsinki Olympics, Frank was hitting the headlines in Sweden, this time for more controversial reasons. His commitment to hard training regimes and his expectation that his players should follow the same strict fitness regime as he did himself, did not go down well in Swedish football, which was only in the process of becoming a fully professional game. His decision to ban his players from drinking alcohol and boxing (perhaps thinking back to those Stoke City injuries in 1939) was headline news in the Swedish nationals in October 1952.

"FRANK SOO INTRODUCES THE TOTAL BAN ON ALCOHOL AT CITY: BRANDY TEARS AT WEEKLY TRAINING" ran the headline in *Aftonbladet* on 3 October 1952, followed by a full page spread on the subject. The original Swedish headline is BRÄNNVIN RIVER NER VECKANS TRÄNIN and is virtually incomprehensible to modern Swedes, but it is clear that there was considerable unhappiness about the new rules. The newspaper asked several local sports personalities to debate the pros and cons of Frank's methods. The consensus was that neither prohibition was necessary. It was not thought that there was an alcohol problem with Eskilstuna's players, most of whom belonged to a temperance organization called the Good Templars. It was also thought that a drink after the match was perfectly acceptable, although, the contributors who were connected with Eskilstuna, Gunnar Malmgren and Per-Erik Nordström, said that they would respect the new manager's total ban on alcohol. Similarly, no one thought that a ban on boxing was a particularly good idea.

Frank's duties also included coaching in local schools, as it had been when he was at Luton and St Albans. He seems to have been committed to this idea and to have particularly enjoyed that aspect of coaching. In October 1952, Eskilstuna announced a project to build a new Sports Hall later in the autumn. The press were convinced that "the little Anglo-Chinese" was behind the plans for the new facilities, as well as being responsible for the sudden improvement of local teams at schoolboy level.

Frank's main job was as Eskilstuna coach and by the end of the season, City were vying for a place at the top of the second division with their rivals Sandvikens IF. "City gives the impression of being a very well-knit bunch," wrote Harald Lindkvist in *Expressen*, who thought it was also possible that they were "most likely to grow into a great team of high class. But it depends so much if [the club] manages to retain its talented trainer and taskmaster Frank Soo, who has done wonders in the short time he has worked at City. When he took charge the team was on the ropes!" The Swedish word that has been translated here as "taskmaster" is *slavdrivare*, and perhaps needs no translation. It was a description that would follow Soo around throughout his time in Scandinavia and, although the context here was one of admiration, his reputation for toughness and for driving his young players hard did not go down so well when his teams were less successful. Eskilstuna finished the 1952/53 as runners-up in the Second Division (north eastern region), just missing out on promotion to the Allsvenskan. Sandvikens took the title, but only because they had a better goal difference.

Despite his success at Eskilstuna, Frank did not extend his contract but instead moved to Örebro SK, a club in a beautiful medieval university city in the central part of southern Sweden. Örebro had just been relegated to Division Two (Svealand region) from the Allsvenskan, but they had been something of a yo-yo club. They had been in the Allsvenskan in recent years and perhaps looked like a more promising and professional set up to Soo. Things seem to have gone badly from the start, however. From being successful and well-liked at Eskilstuna, despite his toughness, Frank, or his training methods, did not go down well at Örebro. As early as October 1953, *Expressen* was reporting that there were problems in the camp. Although the headline denied that there was any opposition at ÖSK to Soo's "moral requirements" - presumably he had continued with his ban on alcohol and other things that he considered bad for his players - the article opened by telling its readers that "Malicious tongues at Örebro SK, have wanted to tell [that they] do not enjoy trainer Frank Soo, acquired from Eskilstuna City, very well." Clearly some of the players had been talking to the *Expressen*'s Stig Hagberg and they had told him they were unimpressed with what was described as his "Moral Rearmament." The reference to Moral Rearmament, which was the name of an important political and social movement all over Europe during the 1950s, is likely to be wordplay relating to Frank's views on the lifestyle habits of his players, rather than an indication that he belonged to that controversial organization however. The rumours of dissent were denied by club spokesman, Bertil Liedström, but his denial was at the very best, a lukewarm one: "It doesn't matter who you have for a coach. There are always some who do not like the person. Naturally it is the same thing with Soo." It seems as if Frank had split the club down the middle. Some players completely buying into his style and training techniques, while others hated it. There were some "thunderous contradictions," wrote Hagberg. Soo would not tolerate any "carelessness" in training. "It may not suit everybody," said Bertil Liedström.

Overall, the *Expressen* report concluded that the situation was not too bad: "All is well on board the ship ÖSK. It was apparently a case of smoke without fire!" Despite the problems, ÖSK finished the season as runners up in their regional group of Division Two, just above Frank's old club Eskilstuna. A recurring feature of his achievements as a football manager would be that, despite his predilection for moving on quickly, he appears to have left many clubs in good shape and they did well for some years after he had gone. Soo was not to stay at ÖSK long either. As early as April 1954, before the season was over, the *Svenska Dagbladet* announced that from June that year he would be the new manager of Djurgårdens IF. He was to replace "Englishman" David Astley (who was, in fact, Welsh) who had taken the club to the top of the Southern group of Division One and the appointment of his successor was "hotly discussed" by the Djurgårdens board who had considered several candidates for the job. Describing him incorrectly as being an Englishman who had been born in China, the newspaper correctly reported that Frank had played for Stoke City and England. In May, Djurgårdens publicly denied that there was any truth in the reports that he was to be their manager.

One month later there was even more startling news. Frank Soo had been appointed as the coach of the Swedish national team. Sweden's Olympic success in London had been followed by third place at the World Cup finals that took place in Brazil in 1950 (although a number of very strong national sides like the Soviet Union and Hungary had refused to participate). Frank's English credentials undoubtedly weighed heavily in his favour, but his success at Eskilstuna and Örebro also meant that he was building a good reputation as a coach. His appointment as national coach was still quite sensational, meriting a full page spread in *Expressen*, complete with a photograph of Frank demonstrating a tackle to his players. The caption read: *"Här ser ni den eminente tränare i aktion under en träningstimme på Eyravallen i Örebro."* ("Here you see the eminent coach in action during a training session on Eyravallen in Örebro.")

It was being reported that George Raynor, who had been immensely popular as the coach of Sweden - he was called "the little English wizard" by one newspaper - had accepted a coaching job in Italy. In fact, although he would eventually go to Juventus and Lazio, Raynor would first become manager of the Gothenburg club GAIS, and in some ways remained a "king over the water" during Frank Soo's tenure of the Sweden post. Swedish football supporters wanted Raynor back, and they would get their way in 1956. Anybody taking on the job of national coach was going to be judged against him and he was a tough act to follow. Once again Frank's long friendship with Kalle Gustafsson, who had played for the Swedish national team between 1908 and 1924, may have helped. The detailed *Expressen* article revealed that Frank had actually been appointed the Djurgårdens manager back in 1950 but had left before he had barely started "for family reasons" - to be replaced by Dai Astley. We can only guess what those family reasons were, but it does seem likely that it was connected with Freda's reluctance to move away from her recently bereaved mother. Again, there was confusion surrounding his supposed appointment at the Stockholm club. *Expressen* suggested that Djurgårdens had changed their minds following the decision of the Swedish Football Association to appoint Frank as the full-time coach of the national team. Frank's own response to the rumours about both jobs was, uncharacteristically, to refuse to say anything to the press at all.

Frank's reputation for toughness became the issue that preoccupied most sports journalists and commentators. He was from then until the end of his very successful coaching career in Sweden, always known as the *slavdrivare*. "One might think that the English school would be 'outdated,'" wrote journalist Bertil Jansson in May 1950, but the new coaches from football's "mother country" were the first to embrace new trends in training. "Frank Soo is a 'harder' type than Raynor," he went on, "and is much closer to the description 'slave driver,' " before going on to quote an interview Frank gave to the newspaper *Fotboll*: "Usually I run with the boys for ninety minutes. Then I try to make that time as intense as possible. Frankly, I think I notice that most Swedish players take it easy in training and rest up. It is against my principles. ... I want them to be tired after training. But at the same time they must have had fun!" No one could ever accuse Frank Soo of failing to warn his teams of what his approach to training was.

Neither was he afraid to put himself forward for the national job. "Sweden has the best materials to become a football power," he told *Fotboll*. "One can safely afford to be optimistic knowing about the enormous breadth that football gradually provides, and that, strictly speaking, every schoolkid messes about with ball games nowadays."

Sweden did not qualify for the 1954 World Cup finals in Switzerland. The Swedish FA did a u-turn on their original decision to appoint a full-time coach and so Frank was also able to start work at Djurgårdens. By the beginning of the 1954/55 season, Frank was to be seen training with his new club. The national daily newspaper *Expressen* reported in July 1954 that it was still uncertain whether Frank would be coaching Sweden for their international friendly against the Soviet Union at the Dynamo Stadium in Moscow that September. "Soo is not so excessively fond of coaching the national eleven, a task that is considerably diffuse and very difficult," wrote commentator Lars "Luck" Carlsten. "He believes that a part-time post as a slave-driver is a very tricky thing to cope with. It is also the Football Association's mysterious attitude. They have shouted loudly for a full-time coach who could devote themselves to the Association's activities undivided. Whereupon, at the same time, they turned to Djurgårdens' coach. I would myself never accept, if I were Frank Soo. How is it possible to train a national team, if one is only going to be around a few days at a time?"

Nevertheless Frank took the part-time post as Sweden coach, presumably with the agreement of Djurgårdens, despite his own misgivings, and those of others, about how feasible it was to do the job part-time. It was a disaster. The friendly in Moscow, in front of a crowd of 90,000, and officially managed by national management committee chairman, Putte Kock, resulted in a seven-nil thrashing, including an own goal. Even the referee, a Mr William Ling of Cambridge, was bowled over by the Soviet team who led 4-0 at half-time, telling the British press: "It was exhibition stuff. The Swedes played as well as the Soviet team allowed." Frank's only comment was one of resigned acceptance of the overwhelming superiority of his opponents: "The Russians were a team who all moved at once. They were too good for our boys."

The following May, Sweden conceded another seven goals when they played Hungary - the Mighty Magyars, captained by George Puskás - in another friendly, this time at the Råsunda stadium in Stockholm. At least Sweden managed to score three this time, and all of them in the opposition's net. To be fair to Frank Soo, these were extremely powerful teams and the Hungarians in particular were regularly scoring huge numbers of goals at this time, including putting nine in Finland's net two weeks later. The match was played in Sweden in front of more than 38,000 people and it did not go down very well with the public or the Swedish FA. As Ashley Hyne wrotes in his biography of George Raynor: "When Russia scored a second 6-0 victory in June 1955, that was the end of Soo. In the autumn of 1955, Josef Stroh was chosen to coach the side, but not before Kock had made a furtive plea to Raynor [to come back]."

In the meantime, Frank was doing much better at Djurgårdens. In the autumn of the 1955/56 season, the first team went unbeaten for thirteen matches with only twelve players. At the end of the season they had won the very highest award in Swedish football and had become champions of the Allsvenskan.

In the summer of 1955 Frank terminated his contract with Djurgårdens IF. It seems remarkably strange that a manager who had taken his club to the pinnacle of league football should not have continued in his job, but he was on the move again. Later the secretary of Djurgårdens, Gunnar Lundqvist, gave an interview to *Expressen* which provided an insight into how Frank had been seen by his colleagues there. After wishing him luck, he said: "Certainly he drove hard the guys hard, we had our leadership ordeals when we had to mediate between overtired players and Soo and certain whinges - but basically it went well and Frank Soo is a man for all seasons [*en alla tiders grabb*] if you take him in the right way. It was not only thanks to him we won the gold that year, but he contributed most." He felt that it had been a combination of Soo's tough, hard driving approach following on from David Astley's clever tactical training that achieved the best results and won them the championship of Sweden. Frank's assistant at Djurgårdens, Anders Bernmar, who *Expressen* noted "even kept in touch with the Englishman," also gave a view on his former colleague: "Frank Soo is totally my style. For those who really want to give something he is an ideal coach - [there is] nothing for stock thinkers. He has the ability to keep running in the workout and ... he is not merciful. His attitude suits us well here in Sweden because we can never achieve that playful style. He demands a lot and when [people] sometimes carp about co-operation, it is not only his fault. He can sometimes be a bit simplistically 'serious' .... He is techically very skilled but he says that players cannot cope with the technical side of the game if they don't have the strength."

In August the Norwegian newspaper, *Halden Arbeiderbled*, reported that Soo was moving to Oslo. "Soo was a bit of a slavedriver," it told its readers, carrying on what was now almost a tradition, "and some of his players would simply not attend training." The report ended with a challenge: "Which Norwegian club would dare take him as a coach?" In the event, the rumours were wrong and the supposedly unfortunate recipients of Frank's training regime were the players of IK Oddevold, a club based in Uddevalla, on the coast of south western Sweden. The same Norwegian newspaper announced the appointment on 21 February 1956, not failing to remind its readers of Frank's slave-driving credentials. His reputation as a tough coach, and the resentment that his toughness caused among players, was becoming something of a monkey on his back.

Frank Soo's tenure at IK Oddevold was as short and as successful as his time at his other Swedish clubs. Division Three in 1955/56 was divided into twelve regional groups and Oddevold was in Nordvästra Götaland. Oddevold finished the season in second place in their group and were promoted to Division Two. The second season did not go according to plan, however - Oddevold finished eighth in a division of twelve clubs - and his resignation was announced at the end of February 1957, although the *Halden Arbeiderblad* described it as a "dismissal," adding that Soo always had very specific views on "things" and that he was "not always the easiest to get on with." He was replaced by former Helsingborgs IF and Sweden player, Sven-Ove Svensson, whose playing career had recently been ended prematurely through injury. It was believed that Frank was now actively looking for a manager's job back in England, but he did not find one because by December 1957, he was back in management in Stockholm at AIK.

Aftonbladet greeted the appointment excitedly. Frank was not going to be in sole control at AIK. It was what the newspaper described, somewhat inventively, as a "national team tandem." The announcement of the joint appointment was illustrated by a photograph of Frank with Putte Kock, perhaps the most famous football personality in Sweden at that time, who had spent almost his entire playing career at AIK, and was to partner him. They had already worked closely together in the national team setup. "AIK let a New Year's bomb explode on Sunday," *Aftonbladet* continued, "and presented its new football management for 1958." Kock was to be manager, Soo the trainer, and Massa Alfredsson, a former AIK right back, his deputy. Frank had been working with Köping in some capacity, but following what the press described as "two months of intensive negotiations behind the scenes," he was moving to Stockholm. He admitted to being flattered to have been asked to join the struggling Allsvenskan club and outlined an ambitious plan to make AIK the best club in Sweden. "I always aim high," Frank told the newspaper. "Without any goal, you don't get results. That is one of my principles." Despite Frank's growing reputation as someone who was "difficult," it was contradicted by Putte Kock who was keen to work with him again. "To be working with Frank Soo pleases me," he said.

"I can tell you that I suggested Soo before I knew that anyone from AIK had spoken to him. We had a lovely time together in the national team and we'll try to replicate that at AIK."

Frank's contract was for two years, a lengthy one for him. It was a matter of days before he was hitting the headlines again with another controversy about his training methods and the strictures that went with them. Many Swedish clubs were not exclusively for football, but combined several sports, especially hockey, handball and bandy, and AIK was one of them. The initials stand for *Allmänna Idrottsklubben*, "Public Athletic Club." In fact Putte Kock was as famous as a former hockey player as he was for football. Frank wanted his players to devote themselves to association football and give up all other sports. By suggesting this, he had inadvertantly stumbled upon a massive problem in Scandinavian sporting culture. Swedish sports clubs were still part of a strong amateur tradition. This was changing and one of the reasons that coaches like Frank Soo and George Raynor were brought in was that football clubs wanted a more professional approach as they moved away from the amateurism of the past. Besides, football was the only sport which made money. From Soo's point of view, part of becoming professional was to become exclusive. Players shouldn't be spending time and risking injury by playing other sports for fun. Frank's problem was that most of his players simply did not have the mentality of professional footballers and although his views generally had the backing of many people involved in the sport, his ideas were, at best, regarded as idealistic, a "pipe dream" as one writer called it. Frank made it clear that, this time, he was willing to make some kind of compromise with the players on the issue and this had the strong backing of commentators like Bertil Jansson who wrote: "*Släpp honom lös och låt honom arbeta utan hämningar!*" ("Let him loose and let him work without inhibitions!")

Unfortunately some of Soo's players at AIK were not as prepared to compromise as he was, particularly on the issue of playing bandy, an extremely popular winter sport in Scandinavia similar to ice hockey but played with a lighter ball and sticks more like those used in shinty. Three players, the twins Björn and Bengt Anlert and "Bäckis" Jansson spoke to the press after their manager had insisted they turn out for football training on Sundays, a day traditionally reserved for playing bandy. The players were furious that they were expected to abandon the game, and their teammates, in the middle of the season in order to improve their football skills. The compromise that Soo offered them - that they could play on Sundays but had to attend football training during the week - was rejected as it affected their handball and hockey schedule. There was an impasse which would not be resolved.

The Allsvenskan was reorganized to accomodate the 1958 World Cup finals which were held in Sweden in June of that year, so Frank's first season with AIK ran from 13 April when AIK drew nil-nil with Malmö through to October with a gap from the last two weeks in May to the end of July. It became known as the Marathon Allsvenskan with thirty-three games in the season and the first part, before Soo and Kock arrived, had gone badly. Things didn't really pick up with the best result, a six-nil defeat of lowly Motala in May, being the highlight. After the World Cup, things began to improve and there were four straight victories, including 2-3 away against IFK Göteborg, but AIK's only other big win was over another relegation contender when they beat Sandvikens IF 4-0 in August. Attendances, which had reached over 32,000 for the match against Djurgårdens had plummeted to closer to 5,000 by the end of the season.

The conflict between Frank and his players over bandy rumbled on and in January 1959, *Aftonbladet* suggested that there might be something more seriously wrong with his relationship with the club:

> Frank Soo is among those to have been called to the first training session and his fans are also in place. There were many who thought he would not be there, but it was understood that he would not give AIK the upper hand by being absent. The deal between him and the club is currently being investigated ... . There seems to be the view that it is for many [people] to decide what to do. The AIK line has been denied in the strongest terms. We outsiders will need patience and await the outcome of the investigation.
>
> Frank Soo was dogged, when he led the first squad out in the slush. Many were called but few attended. Most did bandy or ice hockey training, not only at AIK, but also at other clubs.
>
> 'It's hopeless to [try to] gather the gang before the middle of February,' said Massa Alfredsson. An even dozen players appeared out of the darkness with Soo at the head and they were Mellberg, Nyberg, Inger Bengtsson, Liander, Segerkrantz, Fridlund, Ingevik, Leo Samuelsson, Wallstedt, Westin and acquisitions Gunnar Johansson from Karlstad and Bengt Pettersson from Västerås.
>
> After outdoor training Soo did his hard training in the Sports Hall. ...
>
> It was not just the players in demonstrations. ... [names other coaches] but there was Frank running with the lads.

The uncomfortable relationship between Frank Soo and AIK did not look like being resolved amd, given his habit of moving on whenever there was a hint of conflict, Frank must have been keeping an eye open for managerial opportunities elsewhere, including in England. By chance, some rather bizarre events were unfolding at a Third Division club back home which were to give Frank a chance to take up a long-awaited opportunity to break into management in the English Football League.

Scunthorpe United had not had a particularly illustrious history, but they were an improving club throughout the 1950s and at the end of the 1957/58 season they had come top of the Third Division and were promoted to the Second. The manager who had taken them up, Ron Suart, returned to his old club, Blackpool, and his replacement, Tony McShane, had not done well. The club finished in eighteenth place in the Second Division in 1959, barely managing to escape from relegation. Scunthorpe decided to appoint Bill Lambton, a former goalkeeper whose playing career, largely in the lower leagues, had been badly interrupted by the Second World War. Following what Scunthorpe United historian John Staff described as a "three-day debacle" the Scunthorpe board sacked Lambton and decided to offer the job to Frank Soo. He had not been completely forgotten in his own country and the announcement of his appointment made the sports pages of the *Daily Express* on 8 June 1959, but in what was becoming a pattern, only a week later the same newspaper reported that he was already embroiled in controversy under what seems like a very unfair headline, SOO PAY SPARKS A ROW.

Judging by the ensuing article, it does not seem as if the problem was of Frank Soo's making. He had presumably signed a contract with Scunthorpe in good faith, but it seems as if he was straight back to the days before he went abroad when he had to battle with short-sighted local businessmen and civic officials. The *Express* report, not stinting on the hyperbole, said: "Tomorrow night will be big fight night at Second Division Scunthorpe United's board meeting. The vice-chairman, 67-year-old Doug Drury says he will resign over the £1,600-a-year salary, plus car allowance, paid to new manager Frank Soo. Drury follows director Albert Robson, who quit last week. Two other directors, Aldermen William Pulling and Mayor Alec Moore also oppose the outlay."

The vice-chairman did not hold back on the subject, telling the press that the club simply could not afford Frank Soo. "He would probably be a good manager," he said. "But our gates don't justify the price." Alderman Pulling and the Mayor backtracked slightly saying that although they were opposed to the deal, they didn't know whether to resign or not. It was left to the Chairman of the club, Jack Wharton, to come to Frank's defence: "We are not in the Midlands League now. We're in the Second Division and want to stay there. We need a manager fit for a Second Division club. Soo is the man – whatever we have to pay."

It was hardly an auspicious start to his managerial career in the Football League and it meant that Frank had to do well in order to justify the deal he had been given. He did not do all that badly and his time at the Old Showground is best remembered as a period when the club consolidated and strengthened the squad. Frank brought in players like Harry Middleton, a forward from Wolves, defender Dennis John from Swansea, and Martin Bakes, a winger who came in from Bradford and would end his career at Scunthorpe in 1963. He also signed the centre forward Barrie Thomas, who had come through the youth system at Leicester City, not long after Frank had been there. Thomas became something of a legend during his two spells at Scunthorpe and scored sixty-seven goals in ninety-one appearances during his first period there between 1959 and 1962. One of Frank's attempts to sign a player, Wilf Carter from Plymouth Argyle, came to nothing however, as the *Daily Express* of 18 March 1960 reported.

> A £12,000 deal for Wilf Carter is hanging fire because a train was 45 minutes late. Carter, 26-year-old Plymouth Argyle inside forward, travelled to Scunthorpe for talks with manager Frank Soo. But the rail delays left him with only eight minutes to spare before the signings deadline on Wednesday midnight... And Wilf refused to be rushed.
> Now Scunthorpe are refusing to hurry too. Soo said yesterday: 'If Carter signed now we couldn't play him this season without League permission – certainly not against Aston Villa on Saturday as I intended. So I'm biding my time.'

Given his reputation as a stickler for discipline and punctuality, it is likely that Soo was unimpressed with the attitude of young Wilf Carter, whom he did not sign. Carter remained at the Devon club until 1964.

Among the youngsters who trained with Scunthorpe United during Frank's time there was a 15-year-old Graham Taylor, future manager of England. His father, Tom Taylor, later said that it was Frank Soo who had "encouraged him to take part in training sessions with United, but his successor was not so interested and Graham was invited to go to Grimsby." Graham remembers him as "a gentleman" and an exacting, but extremely good coach. Despite his age - he was now forty-five - Frank still managed to turn out to play in a charity match in November 1959 along with his old mate, Joe Mercer, who was managing Exeter City, for a team called the Soccer Bosses against a Show Biz XI.

Frank did not start the 1959/60 season well. After drawing with Bristol City at home, he lost two successive away matches, including a 4-0 defeat by Plymouth Argyle. Wins were sporadic throughout the season and the highest place in the table that Scunthorpe reached that season was ninth. It was mostly a season spent at mid-table, but after a worrying few weeks hovering around the relegation places in the autumn, the club finished the season in a respectable fifteenth place. It was a tough league, perhaps best illustrated by the fact that the Ipswich Town side that defeated Scunthorpe home and away that season, was managed by Alf Ramsey and the goal scorers were the formidable pair, Ted Phillips and Ray Crawford. Ipswich Town would be promoted in 1961 and go on to be Football League champions in 1962. Phillips scored twenty-five of his 219 career goals that season, two against Scunthorpe, and Crawford's season involved scoring eighteen goals - one against Frank's team. Crawford would score 324 goals in his career. In his programme notes for the match at Portman Road on 27 February 1960, Ramsey wrote "I rate our visitors as one of the most improved clubs in the country. Since manager Frank Soo took over the reins at The Old Show Ground at the start of the season, the football produced by this little club has at times matched the best."

One of the many imponderables of Frank Soo's career is how well might he have done if he had stayed at Scunthorpe United - or indeed anywhere - for longer. He had certainly not had a good beginning at Scunthorpe because of the dispute about his pay and he must have felt unwelcome from the start. Frank put in his resignation in May 1960, apparently "looking for pastures new." Scunthorpe finished ninth the following season, under new manager, Dick Duckworth and fourth in 1961/62, and many supporters gave Frank Soo at least partial credit for helping to establish the club as an important presence in the Football League. Writer and Scunthorpe United supporter, Chris Brader, speaks for many when he says "It's a little surprising he only managed in the Football League briefly. It's clear Soo left Scunthorpe of his own accord and wasn't sacked. I believe he was quite highly regarded and certainly signed some of our best ever players."

Frank left Scunthorpe because he had decided to return to Scandinavia. He went back to Köping, presumably because of his connections with the club through his friends the Gustafssons, although Kalle had died in February 1960. He may have briefly managed the Norwegian club, Frigg Oslo FK in 1961/62. His appointment was announced in the Norwegian press, but if he was at the club it must have been for a very short time. interestingly, Knut Andersen, the player he has signed for Padova was there at this point. In December 1962, Frank briefly returned to England because Quan had died in Birmingham following an aortic aneurysm. Quan had built up a number of businesses including restaurants by this time and may have been in the midlands in connection with that. Frank signed his father's death certificate and gave his address as being in Edgbaston, but it's likely he had just come back from Sweden to make arrangements for his father's funeral. Quan was buried next to Beatrice, who had died of leukaemia in 1954.

Frank spent much of the summer of 1963 in negotiations with the Israel Football Association. Although it has often been said that Soo was manager of the Israeli side, it is not true. He was appointed and was due to take over the post in October 1963, but there was a last minute change of heart, following a disagreement between Frank and the Israel FA, presumably over the terms of the contract. On 14 September, Mr Z. Brim, the vice-president of the Israel FA, flew into London to have talks at Lancaster Gate with an obscure former Leeds United and Sunderland player, George Ainsley, who was given the £4,000-a-year job. Frank stayed in Sweden and was briefly at IFK Stockholm before becoming manager of the Norwegian club Fredrikstad in January 1964. Frank joined the club soon after a highly successful decade in which the club won the league title six times – including successively in 1950/51 and 1951/52. They finished in second place seven times and won the Norwegian Cup four times. As league champions in 1960, Fredrikstad qualified for the European Cup, the first team from Norway ever to do so.

This time Soo had no problems with his squad members wanting to play bandy or hockey. Fredrikstad was the first club in Norway to play football exclusively. However, he ran into the usual problems when he tried to crack down on the players' drinking habits at Fredrikstad. His time at the club has been described as "short and turbulent." The players were in the habit of having a few drinks with dinner after matches. Frank objected and the board reluctantly banned alcohol from being served after matches. The team had a good season on the football pitch, coming second (known as the silver medal place) in the Norwegian *Eliteserien*, or First Division, just behind the Oslo side, Lyn. Still unhappy, Frank fell out with a number of people at the club and resigned early in the autumn and on 15 December he left Fredrikstad for good.

Soo was now being described by the press, quite understandably, as the "travelling Frank Soo." It was as if he could not stay still. He never seems to have been able to settle anywhere after he left Stoke City and his desire to constantly move on appears to have been exacerbated by Freda's death. He was angry with the world, and - although as the media of the time were much more respectful of famous people's privacy, it's impossible to truly know exactly what his circumstances were - he spent much of his later life living alone. Football was his entire world but it was a world where he could find no real place. In November 1964, he moved to Copenhagen to work for Akademisk Boldklub, who had been doing very badly in the Danish First Division, coming second from bottom in 1964. A Norwegian newspaper, *Sarpsborg Arbeiderblad*, said he claimed to have also had "offers from a couple of Norwegian clubs." Negotiations with the Akademisk's chairman, C. V. Jensen, were still going on although things were looking good, the report said: "Soo is a particular gentleman who imposes very specific requirements." The article included what was clearly an unattributed quote from his time at Fredrikstad implying that he was "a very determined gentleman and cooperation did not always go like clockwork." This was the reputation that Frank now had - he was an accomplished but too demanding trainer who cracked the whip - and he was extremely demanding when it came to negotiating with clubs. He had been overlooked, he felt that he had been discriminated against in the past and he had decided to ensure that he got the best possible deal for himself for the rest of his time in football. Unfortunately time is unforgiving to the professional footballer, and as Frank grew older, he did not realize that the reputation he had in his prime was rapidly diminishing. In his case, it was not even consigned to the history books. By the 1960s in England, the name of Frank Soo was more likely to appear in a quiz question that a list of England's greatest players.

Despite this, he appears to have been quite happy with his situation and, in what may be the only surviving letter written by Frank Soo, on Akademisk Boldklub headed paper, to his nephew, David, in April 1965, he described his life in Copengagen: "I have a life of luxury in football, about eight hours a week, good money, my own Volvo sports car, golf, a wonderful town, and of course my old friends in Sweden whom I almost see every day, only an hour with the ferry boat. I have a nice flat in Copenhagen but I am seldom there. I come to Sweden as often as I can. Though fifty-one years old, I am still hard at training, same weight, and can play a fine ninety minutes tough football. So you see, I am very happy with life. I prefer this type of football to that at home, where too many people are losing their heads and do not understand the full, true meaning of playing football."

6

'SMILER'
Denmark, Sweden, Staffordshire, 1962–1991

Once again, Frank Soo's slave driving achieved results at Akademisk Boldklub who finished at a much improved sixth (mid-table) in Division One in 1966. From here, though, his life becomes a little obscure. He may have coached IFK Malmö for a while. He was not at Malmö FF, but he was certainly resident in Malmö in 1970 as he appears in the national census for that year, the *Sveriges Befolkning*. He was living alone. Alan Chadwick, the boy who lived next door to Frank and Freda in Stoke-on-Trent during the 1940s, believes that he worked as a security man in a hotel after retiring from coaching and remained in Sweden in order to claim his pension. It is difficult to imagine how Frank managed to live without any involvement with football. He had given his whole life to the game and now, as for all players, he was no longer wanted or needed.

As late as April 1972 - when he was fifty-eight - he was in discussions once again with the Hong Kong Football Association about coaching a team in Hong Kong. This was not necessarily strange in itself, but according to the *Hong Kong Times*, negotiations fell through because the HKFA were only prepared to offer him a one-year contract when he wanted a term of three years.

While he was back in England on a short visit in May 1975, Frank gave an interview for the Stoke-on-Trent newspaper, the *Evening Sentinel*. He spoke about his fitness and how he still liked to train every day at the age of sixty-one. He talked about his love for Stoke, both the football club and the people of the area, and he also spoke openly for the only time about his experience of racism as a footballer. It is difficult to assess the impact of racism on Frank's life and career. He believed that it had affected his chances of playing for his country and he was in a better position to know than anyone else. Unfortunately he did not mention any specific instances of prejudice or discrimination against him and it certainly does not seem to have been widespread. In the early part of his playing career, his name rarely appeared in print without his Chinese "origins" or "ancestry" being mentioned, but it was more of a novelty than a negative point. Frank, thoroughly English in many people's eyes, was just one of the lads to his teammates. When he moved abroad, he was regarded as an Englishman in the main, although there are references to his colour in both the Italian and Swedish newspapers that may or may not have been intended to be derogatory. It is noticeable that these references, such as the use of the Swedish word "*svart*" (black), increased in the press when he was perceived as being in conflict with local players or clubs. Racism was perhaps less overt in Frank's time - although there are cartoons of Africans in newspapers in the 1950s and 1950s that are truly shocking to the modern eye - but it certainly existed. When the Sing Tao football club toured England in 1947, terrible jokes about "chinks in the defence" were not even considered to be offensive.

Sammy Chung, who was a professional footballer between 1950 and 1965 and managed Wolverhampton Wanderers during the 1970s, says that he did not experience any racism in football, adding "I had more trouble in school!" He does not believe that Frank's Chinese background would have been a hindrance to him, "It never made a difference for me." On a personal level, Chung says that he was inspired by watching Frank play: "I never sat down and spoke with him," he told the *Guardian* in 2013. "That is something that annoys me to this day. I watched him and read about him any time I got a chance. I wanted to follow in his footsteps."

What many British people from Chinese backgrounds find most difficult is not so much overt racism - which certainly exists and is quite open now - but the more subtle form of being rendered invisible. As actor Elizabeth Chan has written, "We Chinese have become dab hands at this, living up to the stereotype of the smiling but silent Chinaman." It is a stereotype that brings Frank Soo to mind. Although it was never in his character to remain silent, he has been silenced by omission (almost) from the millions of words that have been written about football during and after his career, silenced by his almost complete disappearance from a narrative to which he should have been central. In writing this book, it has been the invisibility, the absence of Frank Soo from that narrative that has been the most difficult thing to comprehend. Certainly, his years living outside Britain will have contributed to his having been forgotten, but it does not remotely explain what at times seems like his expulsion from the story of twentieth century football in England.

Frank may have been in Stoke-on-Trent in 1975 because he was thinking of coming back to live there. He retired to the area soon after he gave that interview. He appears to have returned to England alone and, after staying with his brother Norman for a while in Liverpool, he settled in the Potteries. The people who remember him from this time are those who came across him when he was watching football games in local parks. Occasionally he would tell people who he was and show them one of the old cigarette cards that he still carried with him. One of the people who met him in that way was Joe Byatt, a Stoke fan who now lives in Australia who told me: "Growing up in the Shelton area, a load of us used to play football in Hanley Park. This was in the early to mid-1980s. We realised there was an elderly gentleman who would often be walking past and stop to watch us. Over time we would politely greet the man. After one game we were sat on the grass talking and he came over to us and opened his wallet to show us a cigarette card. He told us the footballer on the card was him in the days when he played for Stoke City. From grandparents we'd all heard of a fine Stoke player named Frank Soo so on realising he'd been watching us it was a big thrill! One of us had mentioned he lived nearby but, in the pre-internet days, we had little idea what he looked like. Sadly, a few years on, we would see him in the area and he'd clearly become disorientated. There were times when he seemed to spend minutes at a time trying to cross a road despite no traffic and, in late 1990, it wasn't a surprise to hear he was permanently hospitalized. Hopefully his final years were as comfortable as they could have been."

Several people can tell very similar stories about Frank during the 1980s. The reason that he was beginning to appear disorientated was because, like so many professional footballers who had played in the days of that heavy, laced, leather football, he was gradually becoming affected by a form of dementia. Towards the end of his life, he was looked after at St Edward's psychiatric hospital, in the pretty North Staffordshire village of Cheddleton. This is not far from Wetley Rocks, where Freda was buried, and it's possible that he had either been living there or he was still in touch with members of her family who lived in the area.

A Stoke City supporter came across Frank at this time and wrote about it on an online message board: "During his later years in the late 1980's he was in St Edward's hospital in Cheddleton with my late granddad. My granddad had Alzheimer's, but I'm not sure if that was the reason Frank Soo was in there. When we used to visit my granddad there would be about five or six patients, including Frank, who would sit round this large table. One bloke called Bod would constantly go up to Frank, patting him on the back and shouting 'Frankie Soo, the greatest player Stoke and England ever had!' Frank never ever said a word, he just used to sit there with a big grin on his face."

Alan Chadwick never forgot his friend Frank Soo and having heard that he was now a patient in St Edward's tried to visit him. He telephoned and was told that Frank was suffering from dementia and that in the doctor's opinion, it had been caused by repeatedly heading the ball during his playing career. Frank was by then so unwell that Alan was advised not to visit him. Shortly before he died on 25 January 1991, Frank was moved to a cottage hospital in the nearby market town of Cheadle. His death was registered by his brother, Jack, who had travelled down with some of Frank's nephews to take him home to Liverpool. The cause of death was given as "Right hemiplegia; senile dementia."

Frank Soo, professional footballer, England international and highly-respected European coach, was cremated at Springwood in Liverpool, attended by his surviving family, and his ashes were scattered there.

AFTERWORD

Despite his achievements, Frank Soo disappeared for a long time from the narrative of the history of professional football in Britain, but that is true of many people who played the game at that level. Are there really grounds to justify returning this all-but-forgotten man to a place among the true greats of association football? My answer would be that he deserves to be acknowledged as such on the evidence of his playing ability alone. Contemporary evidence reveals him as having been a delight to watch: elegant, tricky, quick, intelligent, an inch-perfect passer of the ball. These are all things that delight the lover of football now, but they also did back then in the 1930s and 1940s when the game was played with a heavy, often water-soaked ball. It is only possible to speculate about how good Frank Soo would have been if he had played in the modern game.

He was a role model too. His dedication to fitness - he didn't drink or smoke, watched his weight, trained hard every day - is modern. He was accurately described as ahead of his time. Not only that, his position as the first non-European footballer to be selected for England is genuinely significant. The unofficial status of his caps hardly seems important, although it would be justice for all the players who received them for the Football Association to retrospectively change this. The absence of people from Chinese or other Asian backgrounds from football is a blight on the game. Only now that the global nature of wealthy football clubs and the media interest that goes with it sees a huge potential market in Asia is there talk of football in China, Korea, Malaysia or Singapore. In fact, there has long been an interest in football in these countries. Likewise there is a thriving football scene in Chinese communities in Britain. It is only possible to speculate how much of a difference knowing about Frank Soo might have made to young footballers from Chinese backgrounds.

Was Frank Soo up there with his great contemporaries like Stanley Matthews, Tommy Lawton and Joe Mercer? Many of his contemporaries, including Mercer, Dixie Dean and Neil Franklin thought so. Off the pitch, too, he was one of the first players to be seen as a celebrity. Newspapers and magazines loved publishing stories about his life outside football and he had the photogenic qualities to go with it. Although he was not a great success as a manager in England, his abilities as a coach in Scandinavia deserve a reappraisal. He is remembered for his achievements at Djurgårdens but he consistently improved teams at club level and laid the foundations for most of those clubs to continue to progress.

Arguments against his greatness will mainly concentrate upon his lack of goals. He scored very few during his career, although he can be excused on the grounds that for much of his career he played in a defensive role.

He was, by all accounts, an unselfish player. He passed the ball, he linked up with his forwards, he assisted his teammates who put the ball in the net. None of the contemporary match reports that I have seen complain that Frank Soo should have scored more goals.

The final question is: why has Frank Soo been forgotten? He certainly didn't help himself by moving to Sweden for so many years. If he had stayed in England and managed a few Football League clubs, he might not have disappeared so completely. He did not have the same desire to present himself as a great figure in sport as Stanley Matthews did. He also had a reputation for being difficult, although he was no more difficult than many other players and certainly not as prone to throwing his weight about as Matthews was. His regular appearances in the *Daily Worker*, a newspaper produced by the Communist Party of Great Britain, probably didn't help either. Even representatives of the Players' Union were reluctant to speak to that newspaper. Frank was interested in football. It was everything to him. If he thought that something was wrong or unfair or unjust, he spoke out. He stood up for what he believed in and it didn't always win him friends, especially among the wealthy and powerful people who were - even back then - hovering around the game.

No one knows what the slow, destructive impact of dementia - that cruel disease that has affected so many footballers - had on Frank Soo's personality and behaviour, or for how long. Perhaps a twenty-first century equivalent would have been able to spend his retirement regaling us with his memories, but no one was interested in his time, when many professional footballers spent their later years working as plumbers or pub landlords. He did not write an autobiography and gave few interviews. When he did speak, he talked about his only passion, football. He belongs to an age when most footballers were modest, unassuming and did not see themselves as important world figures with opinions on everything from politics to morality.

All of these are reasons why Frank Soo has not received the attention he warranted, but there is no doubt that some of his "invisibility" was because he was seen as being different, other, not "one of us." The irony was, of course, that he was absolutely one of us and if he remained an outsider, it was not a situation of his making. Frank Soo was a shining star in his day and now he deserves a fitting place in our collective memory.

APPENDIX 1

Frankie and Stan

It would be extremely difficult to write the story of Frank Soo's life without mentioning that other, much more famous footballer, Stanley Matthews. They were born within twelve months of one another. They came from rather different families, but they shared many things in common. They both came from working-class backgrounds, their hard-working families ran small businesses in large industrial northern cities - Stoke-on-Trent is actually slightly south of Norwich but in terms of culture it is distinctly part of the North. As footballers, too, their careers had many parallels. They were quite similar as players, despite favouring opposite sides of the pitch. They were both tricky wingers, renowned for the elegance and skill of their play and the pin-point accuracy of their passing. Although very different in character, Frank and Stanley were both extremely self-disciplined, both were described as being fitness "fanatics," neither of them smoked or drank despite being at clubs where the fags and booze culture was rife for much of the time. They both kept in good shape physically long after their playing careers were over and prided themselves on it. Anyone could be forgiven for making the assumption that Frank Soo and Stanley Matthews would have been good, if not close, friends.

It comes as something of a surprise then - it wouldn't be too strong to say that it is astonishing - to discover that in all Stanley Matthews' autobiographies - and he wrote or co-wrote five of them - he barely mentions Frank Soo at all. In fact, Frank only appears in his first book, *Feet First* (1948). His second memoir, *Feet First Again* (1952) is really just an updated version of the earlier one. Matthews did not see fit to refer to Frank Soo at all in his later books, *The Stanley Matthews Story* (1960) or *The Way It Was* (2000). *Back In Touch* (1981) was very much an attempt to justify events in his personal life and did not cover his days with Stoke City in the 1930s and 1940s, so it is less surprising that he fails to mention Soo in it.

Nevertheless mentioning someone with whom he must have had a great deal of contact over a period of about fifteen years only a few times in five books is strikingly odd. Perhaps even more strangely, when Matthews does mention Frank, it is never in the context of playing football. The nearest Frank gets to a football field in Matthews' books is when he mentions Soo having to pull out of an England international against Belgium in 1946.

He is mentioned again in passing as a fellow passenger on a boat train to Ireland which was derailed and the most detailed account of him of all is a story about Matthews, Soo and fellow Stoke City player, Neil Franklin on an England trip to play a friendly in Portugal:

> Sometimes on my travels on foreign soil I am cheered by the unexpected sound of an Englishman – or better still, a North Staffordshire tongue. It happened after this game. (In Lisbon) we were in the bus being driven back to Estoril, and I was remarking to Frankie Soo at the amazing number of cars on the road, adding that there obviously was not a petrol shortage in Portugal, when one of the cars came alongside of us and did not make any attempt to go ahead. Instead, the driver pulled his window down and shouted out: 'We are from Stoke.'
>
> Franklin, Soo and I looked at each other in some amazement, and the driver shouted again: 'My name is Brown, and I'm from Fenton.' He kept alongside until our bus forked right for our hotel. 'See you tonight at the banquet!' He shouted as he took the road straight ahead.
>
> We met him that night with his wife and a friend, and learned he was in the pottery business, and had left Stoke many years ago to act as an agent for the business in Lisbon.

That is the extent of Stanley Matthews' published recollections of his teammate, Frank Soo. Yet we know that Stanley and Frank started their professional career together at Stoke City as teenagers, at an age when many people form close and lasting ties. We know that they ran the line together at charity matches in Staffordshire, and made appearances together at club events. They played golf together along with other players. When the Second World War broke out, they both joined the Royal Air Force and for a time were both at the same recruitment camp near Blackpool. They both played for the RAF, various Football Association representative sides and for England, although of course Matthews' England career was much lengthier and included many more (and official) caps. During their time at Stoke City, they played together in 129 League and FA Cup matches and at least twenty-six games (War League, War Cup and friendlies) during the Second World War. They also played together in eight Wartime and Victory internationals, as well as countless representative matches for the FA and the RAF. They both stood up for their rights when it came to wages and conditions at their club, and both had run-ins with the Stoke's manager, Bob McGrory, something which, if nothing else could, would have been likely to form a bond between two people.

When Matthews does refer to Frank Soo, there is no hint of hostility. He always calls him Frankie, appears to regard him as a friend, but there's little warmth either. Soo is missing from many other footballers' autobiographies but of those who did play with him Stan Mortensen, Joe Mercer and Neil Franklin were all very complimentary about him as a player and clearly regarded him as a good friend. I don't think that Stanley Matthews had any problem with Frank Soo's Chinese origins. In fact, he seemed to regard him as an honorary "Stokie." In any case, Matthews spent years coaching young black players, sometimes putting himself at great personal risk in apartheid-era South Africa. I don't think the question of racism arises. So why is Frank Soo so absent from the Stanley Matthews memoirs?

There seems to be only two possible explanations of this. A third - that Frank's long period outside England from 1951 onwards meant that people forgot him - does not explain why there is so little about Frank in Matthews' earlier books and why there is nothing at all about him as a player, a player that Joe Mercer included in his all-time XI. One possible reason is that Matthews felt some kind of professional rivalry with Frank Soo. They were similar players, although they were never rivals for the same position. In fact, it was probably Soo who lost out when it came to selection for England. One explanation of his lack of chances for England is that he was too similar to Matthews and the selectors didn't want to accommodate too many players of that kind.

The other explanation is that Stanley Matthews' books are all about what his biographer, Jon Henderson, called "the Stanley show." He was a nice man, but someone who very definitely wanted to present a particular image to the world - an image of the greatest star the game had ever seen. In that sense, Matthews was ahead of his time. In reading his autobiographies - the first four are basically rewrites of the same story - it's possible to trace the differences in the way that he wanted to be seen by his public. A few individual stories illustrate this very well. His versions of the infamous Nazi salute that the England team gave before a match in Germany in 1938, the Burnden Park disaster of 1946 and his portrayal of his own family life all change over time in order to present the image that he wanted the world to see.

In the first incident, Matthews seems to have embellished his claim that the players objected to giving the salute. From initially saying that the players felt lukewarm about it - the British Embassy was apparently keen not to offend their Nazi hosts - his later accounts added that some players, including Matthews himself, were furious about the instruction to give the salute and included what can only be described as an apocryphal story that the players were all looking at a Union Jack in the crowd while they gave the salute and concentrating on beating the Germans. The second example was the difference in attitude he displayed over time to the Burnden Park disaster, a shocking tragedy which took place just after Frank Soo left Stoke City in which twenty-three people died. Many people were horrified that the match was allowed to carry on after the crush, in which thirty-three people were killed, took place. In *Feet First*, Matthews said that he and the other players were only thinking of the match and were perfectly happy to play. He sounds remarkably callous, although that probably wasn't his intention. Indeed, in his later books, he condemns the authorities for allowing the game to continue. His presentation of Stanley Matthews, the happily married man turned out to be quite far from the truth too, although his public didn't find that out until many years later. His autobiographies are very much part of presenting the Stanley Matthews that he wanted to show the world: the consummate player, the professional, the family man who was in fact unhappily married for much of his life.

All this may not be relevant to Frank Soo's story but could help to explain why Matthews virtually ignores him in his memoirs. There were many supporters, particularly at Stoke, who adored Matthews but loved Frank Soo even more. Matthews was not the only player to draw in the crowds but that did not fit in with his narrative. There's no question that Stanley Matthews was a truly great footballer, and Frank Soo's flaws, particularly his low goal scoring, meant that he was not on the same level, although many football fans and journalists who watched them both play thought that Soo was his equal and a few thought he was a better player. If was unlikely to have been a conscious strategy to exclude Frank Soo on Matthews' part, but if it was his subconscious desire to diminish his place in football history, he succeeded.

Matthews was something of a loner. He does not come across as being particularly close to anyone. He was not particularly generous about any of his contemporaries, except perhaps to players like Raich Carter with whom he had a rewarding partnership when they played together for England. Sadly, we will never know what his opinion of Frank Soo was, but we do know that when they played together, and particularly when one would assist the other in the creation of a goal out of nothing, they were capable of setting an entire crowd ablaze with excitement.

APPENDIX 2

FOOTBALL LEAGUE CAREER
1933 - 1948

1933/34 Stoke City

DATE	H/A	OPPONENT	RESULT	SCORE	COMPETITION	GOALS
04 Nov	A	Middlesbrough	L	1-6	Division 1	-
11 Nov	H	Manchester City	L	0-1	Division 1	-
18 Nov	A	Arsenal	L	0-3	Division 1	-
25 Dec	H	Leicester City	W	2-1	Division 1	-
26 Dec	A	Leicester City	L	1-3	Division 1	-
30 Dec	A	Chelsea	L	0-2	Division 1	-
06 Jan	H	Sunderland	W	3-0	Division 1	-
13 Jan	H	Bradford Pk Ave	W	3-0	FA Cup R3	1
20 Jan	A	Portsmouth	L	1-3	Division 1	-
27 Jan	H	Blackpool	W	3-0	FA Cup R4	1
29 Jan	H	Huddersfield	W	3-0	Division 1	1
03 Feb	A	Derby County	L	1-5	Division 1	-
02 Apr	H	Tottenham H	W	2-0	Division 1	-
07 Apr	A	Everton	D	2-2	Division 1	-
28 Apr	H	Newcastle Utd	W	2-1	Division 1	-
05 May	A	Sheffield Wed	D	2-2	Division 1	-

1934/35 Stoke City

DATE	H/A	OPPONENT	RESULT	SCORE	COMPETITION	GOALS
03 Sep	A	Leeds Utd	L	2-4	Division 1	-
08 Sep	A	Derby County	W	2-0	Division 1	-

DATE	H/A	OPPONENT	RESULT	SCORE	COMPETITION	GOALS
15 Sep	A	Manchester City	L	1-3	Division 1	-
22 Sep	H	Middlesbrough	W	2-0	Division 1	-
29 Sep	A	Blackburn Rovers	W	1-0	Division 1	-
02 Mar	A	Aston Villa	L	1-4	Division 1	-
09 Mar	H	Chelsea	L	0-1	Division 1	-
16 Mar	A	Sunderland	L	1-4	Division 1	-
30 Mar	A	Everton	L	0-5	Division 1	-

1935/36 Stoke City

DATE	H/A	OPPONENT	RESULT	SCORE	COMPETITION	GOALS
18 Sep	A	Liverpool	L	0-2	Division 1	-
21 Sep	A	Birmingham	W	5-0	Division 1	-
05 Oct	A	Manchester City	W	2-1	Division 1	-
12 Oct	H	Preston NE	W	2-1	Division 1	-
26 Oct	H	Derby County	D	0-0	Division 1	-
02 Nov	A	Everton	L	1-5	Division 1	-
09 Nov	H	Bolton W	L	1-2	Division 1	-
16 Nov	A	Huddersfield	L	1-2	Division 1	-
23 Nov	H	Portsmouth	W	2-0	Division 1	-
30 Nov	A	Aston Villa	L	0-4	Division 1	-
07 Dec	H	Wolves	W	4-1	Division 1	-
14 Dec	A	Sheffield Wed	W	1-0	Division 1	-
21 Dec	H	Middlesbrough	D	1-1	Division 1	-
25 Dec	A	Blackburn Rovers	W	1-0	Division 1	-
26 Dec	H	Blackburn Rovers	W	2-0	Division 1	-
28 Dec	A	Leeds Utd	L	1-4	Division 1	-
04 Jan	H	West Bromwich	W	3-2	Division 1	-
11 Jan	A	Millwall	D	0-0	FA Cup R3	-
15 Jan	H	Millwall	W	4-0	FA Cup R3r	-
18 Jan	A	Sunderland	L	0-1	Division 1	-
25 Jan	H	Man Utd	D	0-0	FA Cup R4	-

DATE	H/A	OPPONENT	RESULT	SCORE	COMPETITION	GOALS
29 Jan	A	Man Utd	W	2-0	FA Cup R4r	-
01 Feb	A	Arsenal	L	0-1	Division 1	-
03 Feb	H	Birmingham	W	3-1	Division 1	-
08 Feb	H	Manchester City	W	1-0	Division 1	-
15 Feb	A	Barnsley	L	1-2	FA Cup R5	-
19 Feb	A	Preston NE	D	1-1	Division 1	-
22 Feb	H	Brentford	D	2-2	Division 1	-
29 Feb	A	Bolton W	W	2-1	Division 1	-
07 Mar	H	Aston Villa	L	2-3	Division 1	-
14 Mar	A	Derby County	W	1-0	Division 1	-
21 Mar	H	Huddersfield Town	W	1-0	Division 1	-
28 Mar	A	Portsmouth	L	0-2	Division 1	-
04 Apr	H	Everton	W	2-1	Division 1	-
10 Apr	A	Grimsby Town	L	0-3	Division 1	-
11 Apr	A	Wolves	D	1-1	Division 1	-
13 Apr	H	Grimsby Town	W	1-0	Division 1	-
18 Apr	H	Sheffield Wed	L	0-3	Division 1	-
25 Apr	A	Middlesbrough	D	0-0	Division 1	-
02 May	H	Liverpool	W	2-1	Division 1	-

1936/37 Stoke City

DATE	H/A	OPPONENT	RESULT	SCORE	COMPETITION	GOALS
29 Aug	A	Liverpool	L	1-2	Division 1	-
31 Aug	H	Charlton Athletic	D	1-1	Division 1	-
05 Sep	H	Leeds Utd	W	2-1	Division 1	-
07 Sep	A	Charlton Athletic	L	0-2	Division 1	-
12 Sep	A	Birmingham	W	4-2	Division 1	-
14 Sep	H	Grimsby Town	W	2-0	Division 1	-
19 Sep	H	Middlesbrough	W	6-2	Division 1	-
26 Sep	A	West Bromwich	D	2-2	Division 1	-

03 Oct	H	Manchester City	D	2-2	Division 1	-
10 Oct	A	Portsmouth	L	0-1	Division 1	-
17 Oct	H	Preston NE	L	0-2	Division 1	-
24 Oct	A	Sheffield Wed	D	0-0	Division 1	-
31 Oct	H	Manchester Utd	W	3-0	Division 1	-
07 Nov	A	Derby County	D	2-2	Division 1	-
14 Nov	H	Wolves	W	2-1	Division 1	-
21 Nov	A	Sunderland	L	0-3	Division 1	-
28 Nov	H	Huddersfield Town	D	1-1	Division 1	-
05 Dec	A	Everton	D	1-1	Division 1	-
12 Dec	H	Bolton W	D	2-2	Division 1	-
19 Dec	A	Brentford	L	1-2	Division 1	-
25 Dec	H	Chelsea	W	2-0	Division 1	-
26 Dec	H	Liverpool	D	1-1	Division 1	-
06 Mar	A	Manchester Utd	L	1-2	Division 1	-
27 Mar	H	Sunderland	W	5-3	Division 1	-
29 Mar	H	Arsenal	D	0-0	Division 1	-
03 Apr	A	Huddersfield Town	L	1-2	Division 1	-
05 Apr	H	Sheffield Wed	W	1-0	Division 1	-
10 Apr	H	Everton	W	2-1	Division 1	-
17 Apr	A	Bolton W	D	0-0	Division 1	-
24 Apr	H	Brentford	W	5-1	Division 1	-
01 May	A	Grimsby Town	W	3-1	Division 1	-

1937/38 Stoke City

DATE	H/A	OPPONENT	RESULT	SCORE	COMPETITION	GOALS
28 Aug	H	Birmingham	D	2-2	Division 1	-
30 Aug	A	West Bromwich	W	1-0	Division 1	-
04 Sep	A	Middlesbrough	L	1-2	Division 1	1
06 Sep	H	West Bromwich	W	4-0	Division 1	-
11 Sep	H	Derby County	W	8-1	Division 1	-

Date	Venue	Opponent	Result	Score	Competition	
15 Sep	A	Liverpool	L	0-3	Division 1	-
18 Sep	H	Portsmouth	W	3-1	Division 1	-
25 Sep	A	Chelsea	L	1-2	Division 1	-
02 Oct	H	Charlton Athletic	W	2-0	Division 1	-
09 Oct	A	Preston North End	L	1-2	Division 1	-
16 Oct	A	Manchester City	D	0-0	Division 1	-
23 Oct	H	Arsenal	D	1-1	Division 1	-
30 Oct	A	Blackpool	W	1-0	Division 1	-
06 Nov	H	Wolves	D	1-1	Division 1	-
13 Nov	A	Bolton W	L	0-1	Division 1	-
20 Nov	H	Sunderland	D	0-0	Division 1	-
27 Nov	A	Everton	L	0-3	Division 1	-
04 Dec	H	Brentford	W	3-0	Division 1	-
11 Dec	A	Leicester City	L	0-2	Division 1	-
18 Dec	H	Huddersfield Town	L	0-1	Division 1	-
25 Dec	A	Grimsby Town	W	5-1	Division 1	-
27 Dec	H	Grimsby Town	D	1-1	Division 1	-
01 Jan	A	Birmingham	D	1-1	Division 1	-
08 Jan	A	Derby County	W	2-1	FA Cup R3	-
15 Jan	H	Middlesbrough	W	3-0	Division 1	-
22 Jan	A	Bradford Park Ave	D	1-1	FA Cup R4	1
26 Jan	H	Bradford Park Ave	L	1-2	FA Cup R4r	1
29 Jan	A	Portsmouth	L	0-2	Division 1	-
02 Feb	A	Derby County	L	1-4	Division 1	-
05 Feb	H	Chelsea	W	2-1	Division 1	-
19 Feb	H	Preston North End	D	1-1	Division 1	-
26 Feb	H	Manchester City	W	3-2	Division 1	-
02 Mar	A	Charlton Athletic	L	0-3	Division 1	-
05 Mar	A	Arsenal	L	0-4	Division 1	-
12 Mar	H	Blackpool	L	1-3	Division 1	-

DATE	H/A	OPPONENT	RESULT	SCORE	COMPETITION	GOALS
19 Mar	A	Wolves	D	2-2	Division 1	-
26 Mar	H	Bolton W	W	3-2	Division 1	-
02 Apr	A	Sunderland	D	1-1	Division 1	-
09 Apr	H	Everton	D	1-1	Division 1	-
16 Apr	A	Brentford	D	0-0	Division 1	-
18 Apr	H	Leeds Utd	L	0-1	Division 1	-
19 Apr	A	Leeds Utd	L	1-2	Division 1	-
23 Apr	H	Leicester City	L	1-2	Division 1	1
02 May	A	Huddersfield Town	L	0-3	Division 1	-
07 May	H	Liverpool	W	2-0	Division 1	-

1938/39 Stoke City

DATE	H/A	OPPONENT	RESULT	SCORE	COMPETITION	GOALS
27 Aug	A	Leicester City	D	2-2	Division 1	-
29 Aug	A	Charlton Athletic	L	2-4	Division 1	-
03 Sep	H	Middlesbrough	L	1-3	Division 1	-
05 Sep	H	Leeds Utd	D	1-1	Division 1	-
10 Sep	A	Birmingham	W	2-1	Division 1	-
17 Sep	H	Manchester Utd	D	1-1	Division 1	1
24 Sep	A	Derby County	L	0-5	Division 1	-
01 Oct	A	Chelsea	D	1-1	Division 1	-
08 Oct	H	Preston North End	W	3-1	Division 1	1
15 Oct	H	Brentford	W	3-2	Division 1	-
22 Oct	A	Blackpool	D	1-1	Division 1	-
29 Oct	H	Grimsby Town	L	1-2	Division 1	-
05 Nov	A	Sunderland	L	0-3	Division 1	-
12 Nov	H	Aston Villa	W	3-1	Division 1	-
19 Nov	A	Wolves	L	0-3	Division 1	-
26 Nov	H	Everton	D	0-0	Division 1	-
03 Dec	A	Huddersfield Town	W	4-1	Division 1	-

DATE	H/A	OPPONENT	RESULT	SCORE	COMPETITION	GOALS
10 Dec	H	Portsmouth	D	1-1	Division 1	-
17 Dec	A	Arsenal	L	1-4	Division 1	-
24 Dec	H	Leicester City	W	1-0	Division 1	-
26 Dec	H	Liverpool	W	3-1	Division 1	-
27 Dec	A	Liverpool	L	0-1	Division 1	-
31 Dec	A	Middlesbrough	L	1-5	Division 1	-
02 Jan	A	Bolton W	W	3-1	Division 1	-
07 Jan	A	Leicester City	D	1-1	FA Cup R3	1
11 Jan	H	Leicester City	L	1-2	FA Cup R3r	-
14 Jan	H	Birmingham	W	6-3	Division 1	-
21 Jan	A	Manchester Utd	W	1-0	Division 1	-
28 Jan	H	Derby County	W	3-0	Division 1	-
04 Feb	H	Chelsea	W	6-1	Division 1	-
15 Feb	A	Preston North End	D	1-1	Division 1	-
18 Feb	A	Brentford	L	0-1	Division 1	-
25 Feb	H	Blackpool	D	1-1	Division 1	-
07 Mar	A	Grimsby Town	L	1-3	Division 1	-
11 Mar	H	Sunderland	W	3-1	Division 1	-
18 Mar	A	Aston Villa	L	0-3	Division 1	-
29 Mar	H	Wolves	W	5-3	Division 1	-
01 Apr	A	Everton	D	1-1	Division 1	-
08 Apr	H	Huddersfield Town	D	2-2	Division 1	-
10 Apr	H	Bolton Wanderers	W	4-1	Division 1	-
15 Apr	A	Portsmouth	L	0-2	Division 1	-
22 Apr	H	Arsenal	W	1-0	Division 1	-
29 Apr	H	Charlton Athletic	W	1-0	Division 1	-
06 May	A	Leeds Utd	D	0-0	Division 1	-

1939/40 Stoke City

DATE	H/A	OPPONENT	RESULT	SCORE	COMPETITION	GOALS
26 Aug	H	Charlton Athletic	W	4-0	Division 1	1

| 28 Aug | H | Bolton W | L | 1-2 | Division 1 | - |
| 2 Sep | A | Middlesbrough | D | 2-2 | Division 1 | - |

NOTE: all three above matches were re-classified as "abandoned" because of the start of the Second World War and cancellation of the Football League.

1939/40 Stoke City

DATE	H/A	OPPONENT	RESULT	SCORE	COMPETITION	GOALS
21 Oct	A	Everton	D	4-4	War League Western	-
28 Oct	H	Stockport	W	4-2	War League Western	1
4 Nov	A	Wrexham	D	4-4	War League Western	-
11 Nov	H	New Brighton	W	4-1	War League Western	-
18 Nov	A	Manchester City	D	1-1	War League Western	-
25 Nov	H	Chester	W	2-0	War League Western	-
2 Dec	A	Crewe Alexandra	L	4-2	War League Western	-
9 Dec	H	Liverpool	W	3-1	War League Western	-
20 Jan	A	Manchester Utd	L	4-3	War League Western	-
10 Feb	H	Everton	W	1-0	War League Western	-
24 Feb	A	Stockport	W	1-5	War League Western	1
2 Mar	H	Wrexham	W	3-1	War League Western	-
9 Mar	A	New Brighton	L	1-3	War League Western	-
16 Mar	H	Manchester City	H	2-1	War League Western	-
23 Mar	A	Chester	D	3-3	War League Western	-
25 Mar	H	Port Vale	W	5-1	War League Western	-
30 Mar	H	Crewe Alexandra	D	1-1	War League Western	-
6 Apr	A	Liverpool	W	1-2	War League Western	-
20 Apr	A	New Brighton	W	4-1	War League Cup	-
27 Apr	H	New Brighton	W	2-1	War League Cup	-
4 May	A	Barrow	A	2-0	War League Cup	-
6 May	A	Port Vale	W	1-2	War League Western	-
11 May	H	Barrow	W	6-1	War League Cup	-
13 May	A	Tranmere	L	5-1	War League Western	-

| 18 May | A | Everton | L | 1-0 | War League Cup | - |
| 25 May | H | Manchester Utd | W | 3-2 | War League Western | - |

1940/41 Stoke City

DATE	H/A	OPPONENT	RESULT	SCORE.	COMPETITION	GOALS
31 Aug	H	Notts County	W	4-1	Southern Regional	-
7 Sep	A	Notts County	L	3-2	Southern Regional	-
14 Sep	A	Mansfield	W	2-3	Southern Regional	-
21 Sep	H	Mansfield	W	5-0	Southern Regional	-
28 Sep	A	Leicester	A	0-1	Southern Regional	-
5 Oct	H	Leicester	D	3-3	Southern Regional	-
12 Oct	A	West Brom	W	0-1	Southern Regional	-
19 Oct	H	West Brom	L	1-3	Southern Regional	1
26 Oct	A	Nottingham Forest	D	3-3	Southern Regional	-
2 Nov	H	Nottingham Forest	W	5-0	Southern Regional	2
9 Nov	H	Birmingham	W	5-0	Southern Regional	-
16 Nov	A	Birmingham	L	6-2	Southern Regional	-
7 Dec	H	Cardiff	W	5-1	Southern Regional	-
14 Dec	A	Cardiff	L	4-0	Southern Regional	-
21 Dec	H	Walsall	D	2-2	Southern Regional	1
28 Dec	A	Walsall	L	5-1	Southern Regional	-
4 Jan	A	Leicester City	L	6-2	Midland Cup	-
11 Jan	H	Leicester City	L	2-3	Midland Cup	-
25 Jan	H	Notts County	D	2-2	Southern Regional	-

1941/42 Stoke City

DATE	H/A	OPPONENT	RESULT	SCORE	COMPETITION	GOALS
4 Oct	A	Chester	W	3-4	League North	-
11 Oct	A	Manchester City	L	4-3	League North	-
18 Oct	H	Manchester City	W	5-0	League North	-

25 Oct	H	Manchester Utd	D	1-1	League North	-
15 Nov	H	New Brighton	W	4-0	League North	-
29 Nov	A	Tranmere	W	2-7	League North	-
6 Dec	A	Stockport County	W	1-6	League North	2
3 Jan	H	Walsall	W	8-0	League Cup Qual	1
10 Jan	A	West Brom	L	4-0	League Cup Qual	-
31 Jan	H	Chesterfield	W	2-1	League Cup Qual	-
28 Mar	A	Blackpool	L	4-0	League North	-
2 May	H	Chester	D	2-2	League North	-

1942/43 Stoke City

DATE	H/A	OPPONENTS	RESULT	SCORE.	COMPETITION	GOALS
29 Aug	H	Crewe Alexandra	W	4-1	League North	-
5 Sep	A	Crewe Alexandra	W	1-2	League North	-
12 Sep	A	Wolves	L	3-2	League North	-
19 Sep	H	Wolves	W	1-0	League North	1
26 Sep	H	Derby County	W	5-2	League North	2
3 Oct	A	Derby County	W	0-1	League North	-
10 Oct	A	Birmingham	L	1-0	League North	-
17 Oct	H	Birmingham	L	1-3	League North	-
31 Oct	H	Aston Villa	W	1-0	League North	-
7 Nov	A	West Bromwich A.	D	0-0	League North	-
14 Nov	H	West Bromwich A.	W	5-1	League North	-
28 Nov	H	Wrexham	W	2-0	League North	-
2 Jan	A	Crewe Alexandra	W	1-3	League Cup Qual	-

1943/44 Stoke City

DATE	H/A	OPPONENTS	RESULT	SCORE.	COMPETITION	GOALS
4 Sep	A	Aston Villa	L	2-1	League North	-
1 Jan	H	Wolves	W	9-3	League Cup Qual	-

1944/45 Stoke City

DATE	H/A	OPPONENTS	RESULT	SCORE.	COMPETITION	GOALS
26 Dec	H	Derby County	W	4-2	League North	-
17 Feb	H	Port Vale	W	8-1	League Cup Qual	2
24 Feb	A	Port Vale	W	2-6	League Cup Qual	1
3 Mar	A	Wolves	W	1-3	League Cup Qual	-
17 Mar	A	Crewe Alexandra	D	2-2	League Cup Qual	-
24 Mar	A	Bury	L	3-2	League Cup	-
31 Mar	H	Bury	W	3-0	League Cup	-
2 Apr	A	Derby County	L	2-1	League North	-

1945/46 Leicester City

DATE	H/A	OPPONENT	RESULT	SCORE	COMPETITION	GOALS
29 Sep	H	Plymouth Argyle	D	2-2	League South	-
6 Oct	A	Portsmouth	L	2-0	League South	-
13 Oct	H	Portsmouth	W	3-2	League South	1
27 Oct	A	Nottingham For.	D	1-1	League South	1
10 Nov	H	Newport County	W	2-0	League South	-
17 Nov	H	Wolves	L	1-2	League South	-
24 Nov	A	Wolves	L	0-3	League South	-
8 Dec	H	West Ham	W	4-1	League South	-
15 Dec	H	West Brom	L	1-3	League South	-
22 Dec	A	West Brom	L	3-2	League South	1
25 Dec	A	Birmingham	L	6-2	League South	-
29 Dec	H	Tottenham H	W	4-0	League South	-
5 Jan	A	Chelsea	D	1-1	FA Cup R3	-
10 Jan	H	Chelsea	L	0-2	FA Cup R3 replay	-
23 Feb	H	Derby County	D	1-1	League South	-
10 Apr	A	Derby County	L	4-1	League South	-

1946/47 Luton Town

DATE	H/A	OPPONENT	RESULT	SCORE	COMPETITION	GOALS
31 Aug	H	Sheffield Wed	W	4-1	Division 2	-
04 Sep	A	Bradford Pk Ave	L	2-1	Division 2	-
07 Sep	A	Fulham	L	2-1	Division 2	-
11 Sep	H	Millwall	W	3-0	Division 2	-
14 Sep	H	Bury	W	2-0	Division 2	-
21 Sep	A	Nottingham For	L	4-2	Division 2	-
28 Sep	A	Plymouth Argyle	L	2-1	Division 2	-
05 Oct	H	Leicester City	L	2-1	Division 2	-
07 Oct	A	Millwall	L	2-0	Division 2	-
12 Oct	A	Chesterfield	L	2-1	Division 2	-
19 Oct	H	Southampton	D	2-2	Division 2	-
26 Oct	A	Newport County	W	3-1	Division 2	-
02 Nov	H	Barnsley	W	3-1	Division 2	-
09 Nov	A	Burnley	D	1-1	Division 2	-
16 Nov	H	Tottenham H	W	3-2	Division 2	-
23 Nov	A	Swansea Town	L	2-0	Division 2	-
30 Nov	H	Newcastle Utd	W	4-3	Division 2	-
07 Dec	A	West Brom	W	2-1	Division 2	-
14 Dec	H	Birmingham City	L	3-1	Division 2	-
21 Dec	A	Coventry City	D	0-0	Division 2	-
25 Dec	A	West Ham	L	2-1	Division 2	-
28 Dec	A	Sheffield Wed	D	1-1	Division 2	-
04 Jan	H	Fulham	W	2-0	Division 2	-
11 Jan	H	Notts County	W	6-0	FA Cup R3	-
18 Jan	A	Bury	L	3-0	Division 2	-
25 Jan	H	Swansea Town	W	2-0	FA Cup R4	-
29 Jan	H	Nottingham For	W	3-2	Division 2	-
01 Feb	H	Plymouth Argyle	L	4-3	Division 2	-

08 Feb	H	Burnley	D	0-0	FA Cup R5	-
11 Feb	A	Burnley	L	0-3	FA Cup R5r	-
15 Feb	H	Chesterfield	D	1-1	Division 2	-
22 Feb	A	Southampton	W	3-1	Division 2	-
15 Mar	H	Burnley	L	1-3	Division 2	-
22 Mar	A	Tottenham H	L	2-1	Division 2	-
29 Mar	H	Swansea Town	W	3-0	Division 2	-
04 Apr	A	Manchester City	L	2-0	Division 2	-
05 Apr	A	Newcastle Utd	L	7-2	Division 2	-
26 Apr	H	Coventry City	D	1-1	Division 2	-
03 May	A	Leicester City	L	2-1	Division 2	-
10 May	A	Barnsley	L	4-0	Division 2	-
24 May	H	Bradford Pk Ave	W	3-0	Division 2	-
31 May	H	Newport County	W	6-3	Division 2	-

1947/48 Luton Town

DATE	H/A	OPPONENT	RESULT	SCORE	COMPETITION	GOALS
23 Aug	A	Coventry City	L	4-1	Division 2	-
27 Aug	A	Brentford	W	0-3	Division 2	-
30 Aug	H	Newcastle Utd	W	2-1	Division 2	-
03 Sep	H	Brentford	W	3-0	Division 2	-
06 Sep	A	Birmingham City	L	2-1	Division 2	1
08 Sep	A	Leicester City	L	3-2	Division 2	-
13 Sep	H	West Brom	D	1-1	Division 2	-
17 Sep	H	Leicester City	W	2-1	Division 2	-
27 Sep	H	Plymouth Argyle	D	0-0	Division 2	-
04 Oct	A	Bradford Pk Ave	D	2-2	Division 2	-
11 Oct	A	Cardiff City	L	1-0	Division 2	-
18 Oct	A	Sheffield Wed	L	1-0	Division 2	-
25 Oct	H	Tottenham H	D	0-0	Division 2	-
01 Nov	A	Millwall	L	3-1	Division 2	-

08 Nov	H	Chesterfield	W	2-1	Division 2	-
15 Nov	A	West Ham Utd	D	0-0	Division 2	-
22 Nov	H	Bury	D	1-1	Division 2	-
29 Nov	A	Southampton	L	3-1	Division 2	1
06 Dec	H	Doncaster	W	2-1	Division 2	-
13 Dec	A	Nottingham For	W	1-2	Division 2	1
26 Dec	A	Leeds Utd	W	0-2	Division 2	-
27 Dec	H	Leeds Utd	W	6-1	Division 2	1
03 Jan	A	Newcastle Utd	L	4-1	Division 2	-
10 Jan	A	Plymouth Argyle	W	4-2	FA Cup R3	-
17 Jan	H	Birmingham City	L	1-0	Division 2	-
24 Jan	H	Coventry City	W	3-2	FA Cup R4	1
31 Jan	A	West Brom	L	1-0	Division 2	-
07 Feb	A	QPR	L	3-1	FA Cup R5	-
14 Feb	A	Plymouth Arg	W	3-1	Division 2	-
21 Feb	H	Bradford Pk Ave	D	3-3	Division 2	-
28 Feb	H	Cardiff City	D	1-1	Division 2	-
06 Mar	H	Sheffield Wed	D	1-1	Division 2	-
20 Mar	H	Millwall	L	2-1	Division 2	-
26 Mar	H	Fulham	L	3-0	Division 2	-
27 Mar	A	Chesterfield	L	2-0	Division 2	-
14 Apr	H	Barnsley	W	2-1	Division 2	-

APPENDIX 3

ENGLAND APPEARANCES

DATE	OPPONENTS	VENUE	CROWD	RESULT
9 May 1942	Wales	Ninian Park	30,000	0-1
25 Sep 1943	Wales	Wembley Stadium	80,000	8-3
22 April 1944	Scotland	Hampden Park	133,000	3-2
14 Oct 1944	Scotland	Wembley Stadium	90,000	6-2
3 Feb 1945	Scotland	Villa Park	64,000	3-2
14 Apr 1945	Scotland	Hampden Park	133,000	1-6
26 May 1945	France	Wembley Stadium	60,000	2-2
14 Sep 1945	Ireland	Windsor Park	45,061	1-0
20 Oct 1945	Wales	The Hawthorns	56,000	0-1

BIBLIOGRAPHY

The Chinese in Britain; BBC radio series by Anna Chen (2007)

Books
Benton, Gregor & Gomez, E., *The Chinese in Britain, 1800-present* (Palgrave-Macmillan, 2008)
Cooper, John & Power, David, *A History of West Derby* (Causeway Press, 1983)
Cooper, John, People of West Derby (*Bellefield Press*, 1988)
Franklin, Neil, Soccer at Home and Abroad (*Stanley Paul*, 1956)
Horsnell, Bryan & Lamming, Douglas, Forgotten Caps (*Yore*, 1995)
James, Gary, Joe Mercer OBE: Football with a Smile (*James Ward*, 2012)
Lawton, Tommy, Football is my Business (*Sporting Handbooks*, 1945)
Lowe, Simon, Stoke City: 101 Golden Greats (*Desert Island Books*, 2001)
            Potters at War (*Desert Island*, 2004)
Martin, Wade, A Potter's Tale (*Sporting & Leisure Press*, 1988)
Matthews, Stanley, Feet First (*Ewen & Dale*, 1948)
McColl, Brian, *A Record of British Wartime Foorball* (2014)
Mercer, Joe, *The Great Ones* (Oldbourne, 1964)
Mortensen, Stanley, *Football is my Game* (1949)
Orr, George, *Everton in the 1940s* (2015)
Smith, Dave & Taylor, Paul, *Of Fossils and Foxes* (Pitch Publishing, 2010)
Walker, Neville, *From Slacky Brow to Hope Street: a Century of Prescot Cables* (Metropolitan Borough of Knowsley, 1990)

SPONSORS & CROWDFUNDERS

I am extremely grateful to the following companies and individuals who helped make this book possible.

Sponsors
Vitasoy
Lyca Mobile
Genting Casino
London Chinese Visa Services

Crowdfunders
Grant Bage
Mark Campbell
Alan Chan
Terry Clague
Amber Clinch
Emma Corlett
Rosa Corlett Green
Kalwinder Singh Dhindsa
Neville Evans
Ella Fletcher Gardiner
Liberty Fletcher Gardiner
Rob Freeman
David Gardiner
Janet Gardiner
Adam Green
Hearnam
Stuart Hellingsworth
Alan Zheng-Phoon Lau
Zi L Liao
Michael Cheng Liu
G Lutz
Sooy3
Roy McDonald
Stephen Moore
StokieTony
Mark Pearce
Alasdair Ross
Mark Rowley
Penny & Geoff Simpson
Alicia Chig Soo
Andrew Soo
Danny Spencer
Nicky Wan
Jennifer Ward
Weng Yu
Philip Wong

INDEX

Milton Keynes UK
Ingram Content Group UK Ltd.
UKHW021825100124
435810UK00012B/813